POWER *in* PRAYER

Books by Andrew Murray
FROM BETHANY HOUSE PUBLISHERS
With Updated Language

Abiding in Christ

Absolute Surrender

The Andrew Murray Daily Reader

The Blood of Christ

The Fullness of the Spirit

Humility

The Indwelling Spirit

A Life of Obedience

Living a Prayerful Life

The Ministry of Intercessory Prayer

The Path to Holiness

Power in Prayer

Teach Me to Pray

POWER

in

PRAYER

❖

CLASSIC DEVOTIONS
TO INSPIRE AND DEEPEN
YOUR PRAYER LIFE

❖

ANDREW
MURRAY

BETHANY HOUSE PUBLISHERS

a division of Baker Publishing Group
Minneapolis, Minnesota

Material in this book has been taken from the Bethany House Publishers editions of the Andrew Murray classics. This edition has been edited and condensed.

Published by Bethany House Publishers
11400 Hampshire Avenue South
Bloomington, Minnesota 55438
www.bethanyhouse.com

Bethany House Publishers is a division of
Baker Publishing Group, Grand Rapids, Michigan

Printed in the United States of America

Library of Congress Cataloging-in-Publication Data

Murray, Andrew, 1828–1917
    Power in prayer : classic devotions to inspire and deepen your prayer life / Andrew Murray.
      p. cm.
    Summary: "A collection of more than 150 daily meditations that focus on prayer, taken from the classic writings of 19th century pastor and author Andrew Murray"—Provided by publisher.
    ISBN 978-0-7642-0931-4 (pbk. : alk. paper)
    1. Prayer—Christianity—Meditations. I. Title.
BV210.3.M855 2011 2011
248.3′2—dc23   2011035592

The titles from which excerpts are taken are credited at the end of each selection.

In keeping with biblical principles of creation stewardship, Baker Publishing Group advocates the responsible use of our natural resources. As a member of the Green Press Initiative, our company uses recycled paper when possible. The text paper of this book is composed in part of post-consumer waste.

Cover design by Dan Pitts

12 13 14 15 16 17   7 6 5 4 3

CONTENTS

INTRODUCTION

Mention the name Andrew Murray and certain thoughts immediately spring to mind: consecration and wholehearted surrender to God; the all-sufficiency of Christ; the necessity of dying to self and yielding to the Holy Spirit; the joy of faith and intimate relationship with Him. These messages, which have gone around the world and changed countless lives, came from a man who was both ordinary and extraordinary.

Throughout Andrew Murray's writings, a common theme occurs: prayer. He continually returned to the need for prayer, its place in the Christian's life, what to pray about, and how to pray. This book represents his thoughts on prayer, gleaned from many of his books. Along with each reading is a related Scripture passage. Use this volume to enrich and deepen your prayer life and "grow in the grace and knowledge of our Lord and Savior Jesus Christ" (2 Peter 3:18).

So Will You Have Power *in* Prayer

❀

If you abide in Me, and My words abide in you, you will ask what you desire, and it shall be done for you.

John 15:7 NKJV

Prayer is both one of the means and one of the fruits of our union with Christ. As a means it is of great importance. All the things of faith, all the pleadings of desire, all the yearnings after a fuller surrender, all the confessions of shortcoming and of sin, all the exercises in which the soul gives up self and clings to Christ, find their utterance in prayer.

But it is not so much a means as it is a fruit of abiding that the Savior mentions it in the parable of the Vine. He does not think of prayer as we too often do— exclusively as a means of getting blessing for ourselves. Rather, He sees prayer as one of the primary channels of influence by which, through us as workers together with God, the blessings of Christ's redemption are dispensed to the world. Ours will be the effectual, fervent prayer of a righteous man, availing much, like Elijah's prayer for ungodly Israel (James 5:16–18). Such prayer will be the fruit of our abiding in Him as well as the means of bearing much fruit.

In promising to answer prayer (John 14:13), Christ's single thought is this: "that the Son may bring glory to the Father." In His intercession on earth (John 17), this was His sole desire and plea; as He intercedes in heaven, it is still His chief object. As the believer abides in Christ, the Savior breathes the same desire into him. The thought *only for the glory of God* becomes more and more the keynote of the life hidden in Christ. At first, it subdues, quiets, and makes the soul almost hesitant to entertain a wish, lest it should not be to the Father's glory. But when His glory has finally become the goal, and everything is yielded to it, it comes with mighty power to enlarge the heart and open it to the vast possibilities afforded it.

—— *Abiding in Christ*

THE SECRET *of*
BELIEVING PRAYER

❖

"Have faith in God," Jesus answered. "I tell you the truth, if anyone says to this mountain, 'Go, throw yourself into the sea,' and does not doubt in his heart but believes that what he says will happen, it will be done for him. . . . Whatever you ask for in prayer, believe that you have received it, and it will be yours."

Mark 11:22–24

The most wonderful promises in all of Scripture are those regarding answers to prayer. To many, such promises have raised the question "How can I ever attain to the faith that knows it receives all it asks?"

It is this very question our Lord would answer today. When He gave the above promise to His disciples, He first pointed out where faith in answer to prayer comes from and where it finds its strength: "Have faith in God."

The power to believe a promise depends entirely on our faith in the One who promises. It is only when we enjoy a personal, loving relationship with Christ himself that our whole being is opened up to the mighty influence of His holy presence, and the capacity is developed in us for believing that He will give whatever we ask.

The connection between faith in God and faith in His promises will become clear when we think about what faith really is. It is often compared to the hand or mouth by which we take and appropriate what is offered. Faith is also the ear by which we hear what is promised, the eye by which we see what is offered. I must hear the person who gives the promise—the very tone of his voice gives me courage to believe. I must see him—in the light of his eye and his countenance, all fear fades away. The value of the promise depends on the one giving the promise; my knowledge of his character and dependability creates faith in his promise. In the case of God our Father, there can be no doubt as to His character and power to hear and answer and provide.

—— *Believing Prayer*

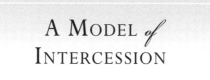

A MODEL *of* INTERCESSION

❀

Then he said to them, "Suppose one of you has a friend, and he goes to him at midnight and says, 'Friend, lend me three loaves of bread, because a friend of mine on a journey has come to me, and I have nothing to set before him.' Then the one inside answers, 'Don't bother me. The door is already locked, and my children are with me in bed. I can't get up and give you anything.' I tell you, though he will not get up and give him the bread because he is his friend, yet because of the man's boldness he will get up and give him as much as he needs."

Luke 11:5–8

*I*n true, unselfish prayer there is little thought of personal need or happiness. If we would be delivered from the sin of limiting prayer, we must enlarge our heart for the work of intercession.

To pray only for ourselves is a mark of failure in prayer. It is in intercession for others that our faith and love and perseverance will be stirred up and the power of the Spirit will be found to equip us for bringing salvation to the lost. How can we become more faithful and successful in prayer? See in the parable of the friend at midnight how the Master teaches us that intercession for the needy is the highest exercise of believing and prevailing prayer. Here are the elements of true intercession:

Urgent need. If we are to learn to pray as we should, we must open our eyes and heart to the needs around us.

Willing love. It is the very nature of love to give up and forget itself for the sake of others.

The sense of powerlessness. "I have nothing to set before him."

Faith in prayer. What the man himself doesn't have, another can supply. To get from God and then give to others what we ourselves receive from day to day is the secret of successful ministry. Intercession is the link between our powerlessness and God's omnipotence.

—— *The Ministry of Intercessory Prayer*

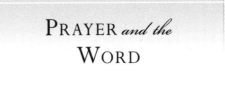

PRAYER *and the* WORD

When Moses entered the Tent of Meeting to speak with the Lord,
he heard the voice speaking to him from between the two cherubim
above the atonement cover on the ark of the Testimony. And he
spoke with him.

Numbers 7:89

With regard to the connection between prayer and the Word in our private devotions, the expression of a new convert has often been quoted: "When I pray, I speak to God; when I read the Bible, God speaks to me." When Moses went in to pray for himself or his people and to wait for instructions, he found Someone waiting for him. What a lesson for our morning watch! A prayerful spirit is the spirit to which God will speak. A prayerful spirit will be a listening spirit waiting to hear what God will say. In my communion with God, His presence and the part He takes must be as real as my own.

As we enter the place of secret prayer, let us be as eager to hear Him speak as we are to say what is on our hearts. The highest blessing of prayer will come as we cease to pray and allow God to speak.

Prayer and the Word are inseparably linked; power in the use of either depends upon the presence of the other. The Word gives you a subject for prayer. It shows you the path of prayer, telling you how God would have you come. It gives you the power for prayer—courage in the assurance that you will be heard. And it brings you the answer to prayer as it teaches what God will do for you. On the other hand, prayer prepares your heart to receive the Word from God himself, to receive spiritual understanding from the Spirit, and to build faith that participates in its mighty working.

In prayer and His Word, God must be everything. Make God the aim of your heart, the one object of your desire. Prayer and His Word will result in blessed fellowship with God, the interchange of thought, love, and life—dwelling in God and God in you.

—— *The Believer's Daily Renewal*

THE ONLY TEACHER

---------- ✿ ----------

One day Jesus was praying in a certain place. When he finished,
one of his disciples said to him, "Lord, teach us to pray."

Luke 11:1

The disciples had been with Christ and had seen Him pray. They had learned to understand something of the connection between His public life and His private life of prayer. They had learned to believe in Him as a Master in the art of prayer—none could pray like Him. So they came to Him with the request "Lord, teach us to pray." In hindsight, they surely would have told us that few things surpassed what He taught them about prayer.

As we see Him pray, and we remember that no one can pray or teach like Him, we agree with the disciples and say, "Lord, teach *us* to pray." As we think about the fact that He is our very life, we can be assured that we have but to ask and He will be delighted to take us into closer fellowship with himself and to teach us to pray as He prays.

Prayer is what we need to be taught. And though in its beginnings prayer is so simple that even a small child can pray, it is at the same time the highest and holiest work to which anyone can rise. It is fellowship with the unseen and most Holy One. The powers of the eternal world have been placed at its disposal. It is the channel of all blessing and the secret of power and life. Through prayer, God has given to everyone the right to take hold of Him and His strength. It is on prayer that promises wait for their fulfillment, the kingdom for its coming, and the glory of God for its full revelation.

Even when we know what to ask, how much is still needed to make our prayer acceptable? It must be to the glory of God, in full surrender to His will, in full assurance of faith, in the name of Jesus, and with a perseverance that refuses to be denied. All this must be learned. And it can only be learned in the school of much prayer, for it is practice that makes perfect.

—— *Teach Me to Pray*

BECAUSE *of*
HIS BOLDNESS

✿

Then Jesus told his disciples a parable to show them that they should always pray and not give up. . . . "Listen to what the unjust judge says. And will not God bring about justice for his chosen ones, who cry out to him day and night? Will he keep putting them off? I tell you, he will see that they get justice, and quickly."

Luke 18:1, 6–8

I t is not because God has to be made willing or available to bless that makes bold prayer necessary. The difficulty is not in God's love or power but in our own incapacity to receive the blessing. And because of this lack of spiritual preparedness on our part, God in His wisdom, righteousness, and love, dare not give us what would do us harm if we received it too soon or too easily.

In the very difficulty and delay that calls for persevering prayer, the true blessedness of the spiritual life is found. There we learn how little we really delight in fellowship with God and how small is our faith in Him. We discover how earthly and finite our heart is and how we need God's Holy Spirit to help us. Here we come to know our own weakness and unworthiness and to yield to God's Spirit to pray through us. There we take our place in Christ Jesus and abide in Him as our only advocate with the Father. Our own will and our own way are crucified with Christ. We also rise with Christ to newness of life, because now our whole will is dependent upon God and fixed upon His glory. We need to praise God for the necessity of persistent prayer as one of His choice means of grace.

Let us acknowledge how vain our work for God has been due to our lack of prayer. We can change our methods and make continuing, persistent prayer the proof that we look to God for all things and that we believe He hears and answers us.

—— *The Ministry of Intercessory Prayer*

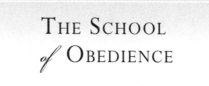

THE SCHOOL
of OBEDIENCE

❁

Jesus then took the loaves, gave thanks, and distributed to those who were seated as much as they wanted. . . . When they had all had enough to eat, he said to his disciples, "Gather the pieces that are left over. Let nothing be wasted."

John 6:11–12

First, let me warn against misunderstanding the expression *learning obedience*. We are apt to think of absolute obedience as a principle, that obedience unto death is a thing that can only be gradually learned in Christ's school. This is a great mistake. What we have to learn, and do learn gradually, is the *practice* of obedience to new and ever-increasing commands. But as to the principle, Christ wants us from the very entrance into His life to vow complete obedience.

This is the reason why there are so many unanswered prayers with regard to God making His will known. Jesus said, "If anyone chooses to do God's will, he will find out whether my teaching comes from God or whether I speak on my own" (John 7:17). If a man's will is truly set on doing God's will—if his heart is surrendered to do it and as a result he does it as far as he knows it—then he will know what God has further to teach him.

Cultivate a strong faith that God *will make you to know* wisdom in the secret place of your heart. Perhaps you have known so little of this in your Christian life until now that the thought appears strange. Learn that God's working, and the place where He gives His life and light, is in the heart, deeper than all our thoughts. Any uncertainty about God's will makes joyful obedience impossible. Confidently believe that the Father is willing to make known what He wants you to do. Count upon Him for this. Expect it with certainty.

—— *A Life of Obedience*

COMMITMENT *and the* SPIRITUAL LIFE

❖

Blessed be the God and Father of our Lord Jesus Christ, who has blessed us with every spiritual blessing in the heavenly places in Christ, just as He chose us in Him before the foundation of the world, that we should be holy and without blame before Him in love.

Ephesians 1:3–4 NKJV

I propose studying the epistle to the Ephesians with a view to discovering the New Testament standard of commitment as presented to us by the apostle Paul. These opening words of the epistle not only give us a summary of the truth of the gospel but also reveal, out of the depths of Paul's experience, what the true Christian life is.

As truly as the blessings are in Christ, so truly is our life in Him. Life and blessing are inseparably intertwined. Abiding in Christ means abiding in the heavenly places and in all the spiritual blessings with which God has blessed us in Him. Faith in Christ is meant to be nothing less than unceasing dependence and fellowship with Him and receiving from Him every grace the soul can possibly need. As absolute and continuous as the contact with the air for my physical life, so is my soul kept in fellowship with the Lord Jesus. This is what Scripture means by the words *Christ is our life; Christ lives in me; To me to live is Christ.* What riches of grace are ours!

Many confess to a lack of a deep spiritual life, and many prayers for its deepening are made. Yet there is often ignorance as to what is needed to bring a foundering Christian to a strong and joyous life in Christ. Nothing can meet our need better than the adoring worship of the Holy Trinity. It is upon God the Father, who has blessed us in Christ Jesus that our expectations rest. It is in Christ that blessing is to be found if we continue in close and unceasing fellowship with Him. It is through the Holy Spirit that the presence of the Father and Son in divine power can be known and experienced.

"I will bless the Lord at all times; His praise shall continually be in my mouth" (Psalm 34:1 NKJV).

—— *The Believer's Call to Commitment*

THE RELATIONSHIP *of* PRAYER *and* LOVE

✿

And when you stand praying, if you hold anything against anyone, forgive him, so that your Father in heaven may forgive you your sins.

Mark 11:25

These words immediately follow the great prayer promise "Whatever you ask for in prayer, believe that you have received it, and it will be yours" (v. 24). In prayer everything depends upon our relationship to God being clear. Our relationship with others must also be unhindered. Love for God and love for our neighbor are inseparable; prayer from a heart that is not right with God or that cannot get along with others can have no real effect. Faith and love are interdependent.

Every prayer also depends upon our faith in God's pardoning grace. If God dealt with us according to our sins, not one prayer would be heard. Pardon opens the door to all of God's favor and blessing; because God has pardoned our sins, our prayers can prevail. The ground for answered prayer is God's forgiving love. When God's love and forgiveness have taken possession of our hearts, we will pray in faith and we will live in love. God's forgiving disposition, revealed in His love to us, will become our disposition as the power of His love is shed abroad in our hearts.

If an injury or injustice is done to us, we must seek first of all to maintain a Christlike disposition—to be kept from a desire to defend our rights or to punish the offender. In the small annoyances of daily life, we must be careful not to excuse a hasty temper, sharp words, or rash judgment by saying that we meant no harm, that we did not remain angry long, or that it is too much to ask of us not to behave in such a manner. Instead, we must seek to forgive as God in Christ has forgiven us, diffusing anger and judgment.

—— *Believing Prayer*

THE IMPORTANCE *of the*
MORNING WATCH

❊

For if the firstfruit is holy, the lump is also holy; and if the root is holy, so are the branches.

Romans 11:16 NKJV

There is gracious provision suggested by many types and examples of the Old Testament by which an hour set aside at the beginning of each day enables us to assimilate a blessing for our work and gives us the assurance of victory over temptation. What cause for praise and joy that the morning watch can so renew and strengthen our surrender to Jesus and our faith in Him that the life of obedience cannot only be maintained but also go from strength to strength.

Only one thing will suffice to keep us faithful in communing with God—*a sincere desire for fellowship with Him.* It is in the place of quiet where we are alone with God that our spiritual life is both tested and strengthened. There is the battlefield where it is decided every day whether God will have all of us and whether our life will be one of absolute obedience. If we truly conquer there, committing ourselves into the hands of our Lord and finding a refuge in Him, the victory during the day is certain.

The superficiality of our Christian service comes from having so little real contact with God. If it is true that God alone is the source of love, goodness, and happiness, and that to have as much as possible of His presence, His fellowship, and His blessing is our highest joy, then surely to meet Him alone in the morning ought to be our aim. To have had God appear to them and speak to them was the secret of the strength of the Old Testament saints.

God has called us to live a life in the supernatural. Allow your devotional time each day to be as the open gate of heaven through which light and power stream into your waiting heart and from which you go out to walk with God throughout the day.

—— *A Life of Obedience*

GOD SEEKS
INTERCESSORS

✿

You did not choose me, but I chose you and appointed you to go and bear fruit—fruit that will last. Then the Father will give you whatever you ask in my name.

John 15:16

There is a world out there with millions who are perishing without Christ. The work of intercession is its only hope. Much of our expressions of love and efforts in ministry are comparatively vain because there is so little real intercession connected with it. Countless numbers live as though there were no Son of God who died for them. Multitudes pass into outer darkness without hope. And of those who bear the name of Christ, the great majority live in utter ignorance or indifference to this fact.

Every soul is worth more than the world and nothing less than the price paid for it by Christ's blood. Each is within reach of the power that can be tapped through intercession. If we had a concept of the magnitude of the work to be done by God's intercessors, we would cry out to God for an outpouring of the Spirit of intercession.

When God called His people out of Egypt, He separated the priestly tribe to draw near to Him, stand before Him, and bless the people in His name. He sought, found, and especially honored intercessors, for whose sake He spared or blessed His people.

Today there is an ever-increasing number in the church who are beginning to acknowledge and prove that intercession is the primary power by which God moves and opens heaven.

Because where there is a lack of intercession there is a lack of blessing, let us turn our eyes and hearts from everything that would hinder God's hearing our prayers, until the magnificence of His promises, His power, and His purpose for this world overwhelms us.

— *The Ministry of Intercessory Prayer*

THE SECRET PLACE *of* PRAYER

✿

And when you pray, do not be like the hypocrites, for they love to pray standing in the synagogues and on the street corners to be seen of men. I tell you the truth, they have received their reward in full.

Matthew 6:5

In the Sermon on the Mount, Jesus gave His disciples their first public teaching. He expounded to them the kingdom of God, its laws and its life. In that kingdom God is not only King but Father. He not only gives all but *is* all. The knowledge and fellowship of Him alone are their own reward. So the revelation of prayer and the prayer life was a part of His teaching concerning the new kingdom He came to set up. Moses gave neither command nor regulation with regard to prayer. Even the prophets say very little in direct reference to the practice of prayer. *It is Christ who teaches us to pray.*

The first thing the Lord teaches His disciples is that they must have a secret place for prayer. Jesus is our teacher in the school of prayer. He taught us at Samaria that worship is no longer confined to times and places, but that true spiritual worship is something that comes from within the spirit and life of a believer. But He still sees it as important that each one choose a location where he can daily meet with Him. That inner room, that solitary place, is Jesus' schoolroom. That spot could be anywhere. It may even change from day to day if we have to move for the sake of family or schedules, but there must be a secret place and a quiet time in which the "student" places himself in the Master's presence to be prepared by Him to worship the Father. Jesus comes to us in that place and teaches us to pray.

God hides himself from the carnal eye. If in worship we are primarily occupied with our own thoughts and exercises, we will not meet Him who is Spirit. But to the one who withdraws himself from all that is of the world and the flesh and prepares to wait upon God alone, the Father will reveal himself.

—— *Teach Me to Pray*

A Man
of Prayer

❖

So He said, "I will certainly be with you. And this shall be a sign to you that I have sent you: When you have brought the people out of Egypt, you shall serve God on this mountain."

Exodus 3:12 NKJV

Moses is the first man appointed to be a teacher and leader of others. After his first call in Egypt, Moses prayed. He asked God what He saw in him and why He would choose him and then what he was to say when people asked him who God was. He argued with God about all his weaknesses and begged Him to be relieved of his mission. When the people reproached him because their workload was increased, he told God about it and expressed to Him all his fears. This was a time of training for Moses. Out of his trouble was borne his power in prayer, when time after time Pharaoh asked him to entreat the Lord for him, and deliverance came at Moses' request.

At the Red Sea, Moses cried to God with the people and the answer came. In the wilderness, when the people were thirsty, and when Amalek attacked them, it was prayer that brought deliverance.

At Sinai, when Israel made the golden calf, it was prayer that averted the threatened destruction. It was renewed prayer that gained them restoration. It was more prayer that secured God's presence to go with them, and once again it was prayer that brought the revelation of God's glory. And when that had been given, it was fresh prayer that received the renewal of the covenant.

Moses was devoted to God, zealous, even jealous for God, for His honor and will. He was devoted to his people, ready to sacrifice himself if it meant they could be saved. He was conscious of a divine calling to act as mediator, to be the channel of communication and of blessing between God in heaven and men on earth.

—— *The Believer's Daily Renewal*

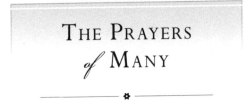

THE PRAYERS *of* MANY

❈

On him we have set our hope that he will continue to deliver us, as
you help us by your prayers. Then many will give thanks on our behalf
for the gracious favor granted us in answer to the prayers of many.

2 Corinthians 1:10–11

United prayer is a great privilege, and its power waits to be experienced. If the believing couple knew they were joined together in the name of Jesus to experience His presence and power in united prayer; if friends believed how effective two or three praying in concert could be, what blessing might come? If in every prayer meeting faith in His presence and expectation of an answer were foremost, in every church united prayer was regarded as one of the chief purposes for which Christians come together—the highest exercise of their power as a church, how might the church be empowered for ministry? If in the church universal the coming of the kingdom and the King himself, first in the mighty outpouring of His Holy Spirit and then in His own glorious person, were matters of ceaseless pleading with God, who could predict what fruit would be borne through those who agree to prove God's promises?

The apostle Paul is a great example of faith in the power of united prayer. To the Romans he wrote and urged: "Join me in my struggle by praying to God for me" (15:30). As a result, he expected to be delivered from his enemies and to prosper in his work. Their prayer was to have a significant share in his deliverance. Of the Ephesians, he requested, "Pray in the Spirit on all occasions with all kinds of prayers and requests. . . . Always keep on praying for all the saints. Pray also for me, that whenever I open my mouth, words may be given me so that I will fearlessly make known the mystery of the gospel" (6:18–19). Power and success in his ministry depended on their prayers.

There will be untold blessing when we meet as one in the name of Jesus and boldly claim the promise that the Father will do what we ask in agreement with others.

—— *Believing Prayer*

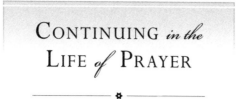

CONTINUING *in the* LIFE *of* PRAYER

❖

Do not let your hearts be troubled. Trust in God; trust also in me. . . . I tell you the truth, anyone who has faith in me will do what I have been doing. He will do even greater things than these, because I am going to the Father.

John 14:1, 12

The Lord wanted to teach His disciples that all they had learned from the Old Testament concerning the power and holiness and love of God must now be transferred to Him. They were not to believe merely in certain written documents but in Him personally. They must believe that He was in the Father, and the Father in Him, in such a sense that they had one life and one glory. All they knew about God they would find in Christ. He laid great emphasis on this, because it was only through such faith in Him and His divine glory that they could do the works that He did, and even greater works. This faith would lead them to know that just as Christ and the Father are one, so also were they in Christ, and Christ was in them.

It is this intimate, spiritual, personal, uninterrupted relationship to the Lord Jesus that manifests itself powerfully in our lives today, and especially in our prayer lives. Do you long to know how you may always experience faithfulness in prayer? Allow God time in your quiet place of prayer to reveal himself and His will to you. The Eternal, Almighty, All-Loving God watches over you, speaks to you, and through you.

Take time also to bow down in worship. Allow our Lord to take full possession of you and to show you how you may live and walk in abiding fellowship with Him. Then you will experience something you possibly have not known before: It has not entered into the heart of man what God can do for those who love Him.

—— *Living a Prayerful Life*

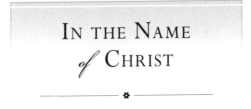

In the Name *of* Christ

---✿---

And I will do whatever you ask in my name, so that the Son may bring glory to the Father.

John 14:13

A name calls to mind the whole being and nature of a person or thing. When I speak of a lamb or a lion, the name at once suggests the nature peculiar to each. The name of God is meant to express His divine nature and glory. So also the name of Christ means His nature, His person and work, His disposition and Spirit. To ask in the name of Christ is to pray in union with Him.

As Christ's prayer nature lives in us, His prayer power becomes ours as well. The measure of our attainment or experience is not the ground of our confidence but our wholehearted surrender to Christ. He says if we abide in Him, we can ask whatever we desire.

As we live in Him, we receive the power to avail ourselves of the authority of His name. As the branch wholly surrendered to the vine can count upon its strength for its fruit, so the believer who has accepted the fullness of the Spirit benefits from the power of Christ's name.

Christ came to earth as a man to reveal what true prayer is. To pray in His name, we must pray as He prayed. He taught us to pray in union with Him. By faith, accept Him as your example, teacher, and intercessor. Just as Christ did, our primary goal should be to receive from the Father. No time or effort is too great to serve others through prayer and intercession.

Be of good courage as servants of Christ. Allow no weakness or lack on your part to cause you to fear. Simply ask in the name of Christ. His promise still stands: "You may ask me for anything in my name, and I will do it" (John 14:14).

—— *The Ministry of Intercessory Prayer*

THE MODEL
PRAYER

❀

After this manner therefore pray ye: Our Father which art in heaven,
Hallowed be thy name. Thy kingdom come, Thy will be done in
earth, as it is in heaven. Give us this day our daily bread. And
forgive us our debts, as we forgive our debtors. And lead us not into
temptation, but deliver us from evil: For thine is the kingdom, and
the power, and the glory, for ever. Amen.

Matthew 6:9–13 KJV

*E*very teacher knows the power of example. He not only tells the pupil what to do and how to do it but also shows that it can be done. Knowing our need of guidance, our heavenly Teacher gave us the words to use as we draw near to our Father. We have in them a form of prayer that breathes the freshness and fullness of eternal life, so simple that a child can learn it, so divinely rich that it covers all we need.

It is an outline of prayer that becomes the model and inspiration for all other prayer and yet always draws us back to itself as the deepest utterance of our souls before God. It is interesting to note that none of the saints in Scripture ever ventured to address God as their Father. The invocation places us at once in the center of the wonderful revelation that the Son came to make *His* Father *our* Father. It encompasses the mystery of redemption: Christ delivering us from the curse that we might become the children of God; the mystery of regeneration: the Spirit giving us new life by new birth; and the mystery of faith: Even before their redemption is accomplished or understood, the word is given to the disciples in order to prepare them for the blessed experience yet to come.

The knowledge of God's Father-love is the first and simplest—but also the last and highest—lesson in the school of prayer. It is in personal relationship to the living God and fellowship with Him that prayer begins.

—— *Teach Me to Pray*

Our Prayer
While We Wait

❖

Let integrity and uprightness preserve me,
for I wait for You.

Psalm 25:21 NKJV

The prayer of our text is one of great importance to our spiritual life. We must draw near to God with a true heart. And to meet with the Holy One, our heart must be wholly given over to His will.

If in our first attempt to truly live a life of waiting on God we discover how much we are lacking in integrity, we can count this as one of the blessings of our attempt. A soul cannot seek close fellowship with God or attain to a conscious waiting on Him without an entire surrender to His will.

It is not only in connection with the prayer of our text but also with every prayer that surrender to His will is appropriate. It must also be clear *what* we are waiting for, not simply that we are waiting. It may be that we long for a sense of His holy presence and nearness. Or we may have a special petition for which we need a precise answer. Perhaps our whole inner life thirsts for a manifestation of God's power. Beyond our own needs, we may pray for the state of the church and God's people at home, or some part of His global work. It is good that we sometimes take stock of exactly what we are waiting for and then renew our intention to wait only on *Him* for the answer.

This brings us to think about *on whom* we are waiting—not an idol or a god we have conjured up by our poor concept of who He is, but on the living God, infinite in holiness, power, wisdom, goodness, and love. Be still and wait and worship until you sense His nearness. Then confirm, "It is on *you* alone that I wait."

—— *Waiting on God*

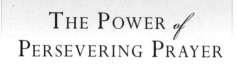

THE POWER *of* PERSEVERING PRAYER

❋

He spoke a parable to them, that men always ought to pray and not lose heart, saying: "There was in a certain city a judge who did not fear God nor regard man. Now there was a widow in that city; and she came to him, saying, 'Get justice for me from my adversary.' And he would not for a while; but afterward he said within himself, 'Though I do not fear God nor regard man, yet because this widow troubles me I will avenge her, lest by her continual coming she weary me.' "

Luke 18:1–5 NKJV

One of the greatest mysteries of prayer is the need for perseverance. That our loving Lord, so longing to bless, should have to be sought time after time before the answer comes is not easy to understand. It is also one of the greatest practical difficulties in the exercise of believing prayer. When even after persevering supplication our prayer seems to remain unanswered, it is easy for our pampered flesh (with all the appearance of pious submission) to think that it must stop praying because God may have a reason for withholding the answer.

The difficulty is overcome by faith alone. When faith has taken its stand on God's Word and has yielded itself to the leading of the Spirit to seek only God's will and honor in its prayer, it should not be discouraged by delay. We know from Scripture that the power of believing prayer is irresistible; *real faith can never be disappointed.* Faith knows not a single believing prayer fails to have its effect in heaven; each has influence and is treasured up to work out an answer in due time to the one who perseveres to the end.

Even as Abraham through so many years in hope believed against hope and then through faith *and patience* inherited the promise, faith believes that the long-suffering of the Lord is salvation, *waiting* and *pressing on* until the coming of the Lord to fulfill His promise.

—— *Believing Prayer*

GOD'S THOUGHTS
and OUR THOUGHTS

———— ✱ ————

As the heavens are higher than the earth, so are my ways higher than your ways and my thoughts than your thoughts.

Isaiah 55:9

The words of a wise man often mean something different than what the casual hearer understands them to mean. It is easy to see, then, how the words of God often mean something infinitely higher than we initially comprehend. Remembering this will prevent our being content with our knowledge and thoughts concerning the Word of God. Instead, we will wait on God to know His mind. Our prayer for the Holy Spirit's teaching will reveal to us what our heart has not yet conceived. It will fortify the hope that there is even in this life a fulfillment beyond our highest thoughts.

Faith in the Word should teach us two lessons: one of ignorance, the other of expectation. We should learn to come to the Word as little children. Jesus said, "I praise you, Father, Lord of heaven and earth, because you have hidden these things from the wise and learned, and revealed them to little children" (Matthew 11:25). The prudent and the wise are not necessarily hypocrites or enemies. Many of God's children, who by neglecting to continually cultivate a childlike spirit and by resting on their creed or personal Bible study, have spiritual truth hidden from them and never become spiritual adults. Allow a deep sense of your own lack of knowledge and a general distrust in your own power to understand the things of God to characterize your Bible study.

The greater our distrust of our own comprehension of the thoughts of God, the greater our expectation will be. The Holy Spirit is in us to reveal the things of God. In answer to our humble believing prayer, God will, through Him, give ever-increasing insight into the mystery of God—our union and resemblance to Christ, His living in us, and our being as He was in this world.

—— *The Believer's Daily Renewal*

Divine
Ownership

---- ✿ ----

*Do you not know that your body is a temple of the Holy Spirit, who
is in you, whom you have received from God? You are not your own;
you were bought at a price. Therefore honor God with your body.*

1 Corinthians 6:19–20

Here is the error that lies at the root of so much of our Christianity. A
man thinks, "I have my business and family responsibilities and my duties as
a citizen, and I cannot change this. Am I to take on more work and service in
the church so that I can be kept from sin? God help me!"

No, it is not like that. When Christ came to earth, He bought us, sinners
that we are, with His blood. If there were a slave market today and I were
to buy a slave, I would take that slave away to my own house from his old
surroundings, and he would live at my house as my personal property. And
if he were a faithful slave, he would live as having no will and no interests
of his own, his one concern being to promote the well-being and honor of
his master. And in like manner I, who have been bought with the precious
blood of Christ, have been bought to live every day with one thought: *How
can I please my Master?*

We find the Christian life difficult because we seek for God's blessing
while we live according to our own will. We make our own plans and choose
our own work, and then we ask the Lord Jesus to watch and see that sin does
not overtake us and that we do not wander too far from the path. But our
relationship to Jesus ought to be such that we are entirely at His disposal.
Every day we should go to Him first, humbly and straightforwardly, and say,
"Lord, is there anything in me that is not according to your will, that has not
been ordered by you, or that is not entirely given over to you? What would
you have me do today?"

—— *Divine Healing*

IS PRAYERLESSNESS SIN?

❖

Far be it from me that I should sin against the Lord by failing to pray for you.

1 Samuel 12:23

*A*ny deep quickening of the spiritual life of the church will always be accompanied by a deeper sense of sin. Jesus is our Savior from sin. To see that our prayerlessness is sin is the first step toward a true and divine deliverance.

What we need is a revelation from God that our lack of prayer is an indication of unfaithfulness to our vow of consecration in which we gave God all our heart and life. We must see that prayerlessness, with the excuses we make for it, is a greater sin than we thought. It means that we have little taste or desire for fellowship with God. It shows that our faith rests more on our own work and efforts than on the power of God. It shows we have little sense of the heavenly blessing God waits to shower upon us. It means we are not ready to sacrifice the ease and confidence of the flesh for persistent pleading before God. It shows that the spirituality of our life and our abiding in Christ is too weak to allow us to prevail in prayer.

When the pressure of work for Christ becomes the excuse for our not finding time to seek and secure His presence and power, it proves we have no proper sense of our absolute dependence upon God. There is obviously no grasp of the divine work of God in which we are only His instruments.

God never speaks to His people of sin except with a view to saving them from it. The same power that condemns sin, if humbly yielded to, will give us the power to rise up and overcome it.

Let us not be afraid, and let us not cling to the excuses and explanations that circumstances suggest. But rather let us confess, "We have sinned; we are sinning; we dare not sin any longer."

—— *The Ministry of Intercessory Prayer*

THE CERTAINTY *of an* ANSWER *to* PRAYER

❊

Ask and it will be given to you; seek and you will find; knock and the door will be opened to you. For everyone who asks receives; he who seeks finds; and to him who knocks, the door will be opened.

Matthew 7:7–8

Our Lord speaks of prayer in the Sermon on the Mount. In Matthew 6, He told about the Father who is to be found in secret and rewards openly, and He gave us the pattern prayer (vv. 5–15). Here He wants to teach us what all of Scripture considers the most important thing about prayer: that it be heard and answered. He uses words that mean almost the same thing, and each time He repeats the promise distinctly: "It *will* be given to you; you *will* find; the door *will* be opened to you." Through repetition, we see that He wants to implant in our minds the truth that we may—and must—confidently expect an answer to our prayer. Next to the revelation of the Father's love, there is no more important lesson in the whole school of prayer than this: Everyone that asks receives.

Some variation of meaning has been sought in the three words *ask, seek,* and *knock.* The first, *ask,* refers to the gifts we pray for. But I may ask for and receive a gift without the Giver. *Seek* is the word Scripture uses when speaking of looking for God himself. Christ assures me that I can find God. But it is not enough to find God in a time of need without also coming into an abiding fellowship with Him. *Knock* speaks of being admitted to dwell with Him and in Him. Asking and receiving the gift thus leads to seeking and finding the Giver. This again leads to the knocking and opening of the door to the Father's home and to His love. One thing is sure: The Lord wants us to believe with certainty that asking, seeking, and knocking will not be in vain.

—— *Teach Me to Pray*

PETER'S
REPENTANCE

❋

The Lord turned and looked straight at Peter. Then Peter remembered the word the Lord had spoken to him: "Before the rooster crows today, you will disown me three times." And he went outside and wept bitterly.

Luke 22:61–62

This was the turning point in Peter's life. Christ had said to him, "You cannot follow me now." Peter was not able to follow Christ because he had not come to the end of himself. But when he realized what he had done and how Christ's prophecy of his actions had come true, he wept. This is the point at which the great change came about. Jesus had previously said to him, "When you are converted, strengthen your brethren." At this new revelation of himself, Peter was converted from self to Christ.

I thank God for the story of Peter. I know of no other man in the Bible who gives greater comfort to the human frame. When we look at his character, so full of failures, and at what Christ made him by the power of the Holy Spirit, there is hope for every one of us. But remember that before Christ could fill Peter with the Holy Spirit and make him a new creation, Peter had to humble himself and admit his sin.

It is the story of every servant who will be truly used by God. Peter's story is a prophecy of what each of us can receive from God. We must not only pray for God's work and speak about it among ourselves, not only pray for an outpouring of the Spirit of love, but we must humbly come to God as individuals in repentance and faith. For it is only when individual servants are blessed of God that the work will prosper and the body of Christ will be strong and fruitful.

—— *Absolute Surrender*

THE INFINITE
FATHERLINESS *of* GOD

Which of you, if his son asks for bread, will give him a stone? Or if he asks for a fish, will give him a snake? If you, then, though you are evil, know how to give good gifts to your children, how much more will your Father in heaven give good gifts to those who ask him!

Matthew 7:9–11

Our Lord confirms further what He said of the certainty of an answer to prayer. To remove all doubt and show us on what sure ground His promise rests, He appeals to a truth all have seen and experienced here on earth. We were all children, and know what we expected of our fathers. It is the most natural thing for a father to hear his child and to give him the best he can. The Lord asks us to look up from our earthly parents—of whom the best are but human—and to calculate *how much more* the heavenly Father will give good gifts to them that ask Him. Jesus shows us that to the degree that God is greater than sinful men, so should we base our assurance that God will grant our childlike petitions. As God is to be trusted more than men, *so much more certainly* will our prayer be heard of our Father in heaven.

This parable is simple and intelligible. Equally deep and spiritual is the teaching it contains. The Lord reminds us that the prayer of a child of God is influenced entirely by the relationship he has with his Parent. Prayer can exert that influence only when the child is living and walking in a loving relationship in the home and in the service of the Father. The power of the promise "Ask and it will be given to you" (Matthew 7:7) lies in that good relationship. Then the prayer of faith and its answer will be the natural result. Today the lesson is this: Live as a child of God and you may pray as a child with complete certainty of an answer.

—— *Teach Me to Pray*

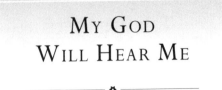

My God Will Hear Me

But as for me, I watch in hope for the Lord, I wait for God my Savior; my God will hear me.

Micah 7:7

The power of prayer rests in the faith that God hears our prayers. It is this faith that gives us courage to pray; that gives us power to prevail with God. The moment I am assured that God hears me, I feel drawn to pray and to persevere in prayer. I feel strong to claim and to take by faith the answer God gives. One of the great reasons for a lack of prayer is the lack of a living, joyous assurance that God hears us. If only we could get a vision of the living God waiting with open arms to grant our request. Wouldn't we then set aside everything to make time and space for the prayer of faith?

When a man can and does declare in living faith, "My God will hear me!" surely nothing will keep him from prayer. He knows that what he cannot do on earth can and will be done for him in heaven. Let us kneel in quietness before God and wait on Him until He reveals himself as the God who hears.

Christ sits at the right hand of the Father making intercession for us. God *delights* in hearing our prayers. He has allowed us to be tried many times so that we might be compelled to cry out to Him and to know Him as the God who hears prayer.

Ordinary and insignificant though I am, filling a very small place in His kingdom, even I have access to this infinite God with the confidence that He hears me.

What a blessed prospect indeed—every earthly and spiritual anxiety exchanged for the peace of God, who cares for all and hears our prayers. What a blessed prospect in my work of prayer—to know that even when the answer is delayed and there is a call for patient, persevering prayer, the truth remains the same: Our God hears us.

—— *The Ministry of Intercessory Prayer*

BOLDNESS *in* PRAYER

❋

This is the confidence we have in approaching God: that if we ask anything according to his will, he hears us. And if we know that he hears us—whatever we ask—we know that we have what we asked of him.

1 John 5:14–15

Undoubtedly one of the greatest hindrances to believing prayer is this: Many do not know if what they ask is in harmony with the will of God. As long as they are in doubt on this point, they cannot have the boldness to ask in the assurance that they will receive. And they soon begin to think that if they have made known their requests and receive no answer, it is best to leave it to God to do according to His good pleasure. The words of John, "If we ask anything *according to his will,* he hears us," as they understand them, make answers to prayer impossible because they cannot be sure what the will of God is. They think of God's will as His hidden counsel. How can man fathom what may be the purpose of the All-Wise God?

However, this is the very opposite of what John was aiming at. He wanted to stir us to boldness, to full assurance of faith in prayer so that we could say, "Father, you know and I know that I am asking according to your will, and I know that you hear me." So this is the basis of our confidence. As we approach God and ask according to His will as we know it, He will hear us. And additionally, if we know that He hears us, we know that through faith we have what we ask of Him.

John assumes that when we pray we first find out if our prayers are according to the will of God. They may be according to God's will and yet not be answered at once, or they may not be answered without persevering prayer. To encourage us to persevere and be strong in faith, He tells us that if we ask anything according to His will, He hears us.

—— *Teach Me to Pray*

THE
THRICE-HOLY ONE

✦

I saw the Lord seated on a throne, high and exalted, and the train
of his robe filled the temple. Above him were seraphs. . . . And they
were calling to one another: "Holy, holy, holy is the Lord Almighty;
the whole earth is full of his glory."

Isaiah 6:1–3

*N*ot only on earth but also in heaven is the holiness of God His chief and most glorious attribute. And the highest inspiration of adoration and praise mentions His holiness. The brightest of living beings, they who are ever before and around and above the throne, find their glory in adoring and proclaiming the holiness of God. Surely for us too there can be no higher honor than to study and know, to worship and adore, and to proclaim and show forth the glory of the Thrice-Holy One.

The threefold repetition of *holy* by the church of Christ has at all times been connected with the Holy Trinity. The song of the living creatures around the throne (Revelation 4) is evidence of this. There we find it followed by the adoration of Him who was and is and is to come, the Almighty: the Eternal Source, the present manifestation in the Son, the future perfecting of the revelation of God in the Spirit's work in His church.

The Trinity teaches us that God has revealed himself in two ways. The Son is the form of God, His manifestation as He shows himself to man, the image in which His unseen glory is embodied and to which man is to be conformed. The Spirit is the power of God working in man and leading him into that image. In Jesus, He who had been in the form of God took the form of man, and the Divine Holiness was literally manifested in the form of a human life and the members of a human body.

Holy, holy, holy, the Lord God Almighty! which was and is and is to come! I worship you as the Triune God. With face veiled and feet covered, I would bow in deep humility and silence, till your mercy lifts me as on eagles' wings to behold your glory.

— *The Path to Holiness*

DAY *by* DAY

❀

In the desert the whole community grumbled against Moses and Aaron. The Israelites said to them, "If only we had died by the Lord's hand in Egypt! There we sat around pots of meat and ate all the food we wanted, but you have brought us out into this desert to starve this entire assembly to death." Then the Lord said to Moses, "I will rain down bread from heaven for you. The people are to go out each day and gather enough for that day."

Exodus 16:2—4

*E*nough for that day: Such was the rule for God's giving and man's receiving of provision in the wilderness. It is still the law in all the dealings of God's grace with His children. A clear insight into the beauty and application of this arrangement is a wonderful help in understanding how one who feels himself utterly weak can have the confidence and the perseverance to hold on through all his earthly years. A patient who had been in a serious accident asked the doctor, "How long will I have to lie here?" The answer came, "Only a day at a time." God's grace is enough; His provision is enough for each day.

Only today is ours; tomorrow is the Father's alone. The question has been asked, "What security do you have that you will always abide in Jesus?" We need not ask it. Just as manna for food and strength was given only for the day, to faithfully fill up the present is our only security for the future. Accept, enjoy, and fulfill with your whole heart the part you have to perform this day. His presence and grace enjoyed today will remove all doubt as to whether you can entrust tomorrow to Him as well.

We begin to number our days not from the sun's rising, or by the work we do or the food we eat, but by the daily renewal of the miracle and blessing of daily fellowship with Him who is the life and the light of the world.

—— *Abiding in Christ*

VICTORY OVER
PRAYERLESSNESS

———————— ✿ ————————

*If we confess our sins, he is faithful and just and will forgive us
our sins and purify us from all unrighteousness.*

1 John 1:9

The greatest stumbling block to victory over prayerlessness is the thought that we will never obtain the blessing of deliverance from it. We may have tried, but in vain. The changes needed seem too great and too difficult. If the question is put to us, "Is a change possible?" our heart says, "For me it is entirely impossible!" Do you know why our answer is such? It is because we have heard the call to prayer as the voice of Moses and a command of the law. Remember this: Moses and his law have never given anyone the power to obey.

Do you really long for the courage to believe that deliverance from a prayerless life is possible and can become a reality? Then you must learn the great lesson that such deliverance is included in the redemption that is ours in Christ Jesus. It is one of the blessings of the new covenant that God imparts to you through Christ.

My prayer life must be brought entirely under the control of Christ and His love. Then for the first time prayer will become what it should be: the natural and joyous breathing of the spiritual life by which the heavenly atmosphere is inhaled and then exhaled in prayer.

Do you see that when this faith is a part of us, the call to a life of prayer that pleases God will be a welcome one? The call to repent of the sin of prayerlessness will not be responded to by a sigh of helplessness or by the unwillingness of the flesh. The voice of the Father will be heard as He sets before us a widely opened door and receives us into blessed fellowship with Him.

By His blood and through His grace there is complete deliverance from all unrighteousness and from prayerlessness. Praise His name forever!

—— *Living a Prayerful Life*

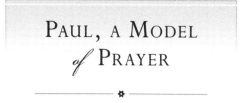

PAUL, A MODEL *of* PRAYER

❋

The Lord told him, "Go to the house of Judas on Straight Street and ask for a man from Tarsus named Saul, for he is praying."

Acts 9:11

Our Lord took Paul, a man of like passions with ourselves, and made him a model of what Christ could do for one who called himself the chief of sinners. The words our Lord used of him at his conversion, "He is praying," may be taken as the keynote of Paul's life. The heavenly vision that brought him to his knees ruled his life ever after. Christ at the right hand of God, in whom we are blessed with all spiritual blessings, was everything to Paul. Prayer and the expectation of heavenly power in his work and on his work were the simple outcomes of Paul's faith in the Glorified One.

Paul had such a sense that everything must come from above, and such a faith that it would come in answer to prayer, that prayer was neither a duty nor a burden. It was the natural turning of the heart to the only place from where it could possibly obtain what it sought for others. This is the pattern Paul followed: First, come every day empty-handed and receive from God the supply of the Spirit in intercession. Then impart what has come to you to others.

Paul's requests for prayer are no less instructive than his own prayers for the saints. They show that he does not count prayer a special prerogative of an apostle; he invites the humblest and simplest believer to claim his right. They prove that he doesn't think only the new converts or weak Christians need prayer; he himself, as a member of the body, is dependent upon his brethren and their prayers.

We have the Holy Spirit, who brings the Christ-life into our hearts to prepare us for this work. As we set aside time each day for intercession, and count upon the Spirit's enabling power, confidence will grow that we can, in our own measure, follow Paul even as he followed Christ.

—— *The Ministry of Intercessory Prayer*

GOD'S DESIRE
for the SICK

——— ✿ ———

Is any one of you sick? He should call the elders of the church to pray over him and anoint him with oil in the name of the Lord. And the prayer offered in faith will make the sick person well; the Lord will raise him up. If he has sinned, he will be forgiven.

James 5:14–15

*S*ickness and its consequences abound in the world. What joy, then, for the believer to learn from the Word of God the way to healing. The Bible teaches us that it is the will of God to see His children well.

Suffering that may arise from various exterior causes is the portion of every person, including the Christian. There is a great difference between suffering and sickness. The Lord Jesus spoke of suffering as being necessary, as being allowed and blessed of God, while He says of sickness that it ought to be cured. All other suffering comes to us from without, and will cease only when Jesus triumphs over the sin and evil that are in the world. Sickness is an evil that afflicts the body itself. When we are saved by Christ, we become the temple of the Holy Spirit. By faith we have the very life of Jesus.

The direction in Scripture given to the one who is sick is to call for the elders of the church and to ask them to anoint him and to pray for him. In the New Testament, the elders were the pastors and leaders of the churches, called to the ministry because they were filled with the Holy Spirit and were known for their holiness and their faith. They were representatives of the church, the collective body of Christ, and it is the communion of believers that invites the Spirit to act with power.

——— *Divine Healing*

CHRIST
OUR SACRIFICE

❄

He went a little farther, and fell on the ground, and prayed that
if it were possible, the hour might pass from Him. And He said,
"Abba, Father, all things are possible for You. Take this cup away
from Me; nevertheless, not what I will, but what You will."

Mark 14:35–36 NKJV

What a contrast within the space of a few hours! What a transition from the quietness of "Father, the time has come" (John 17:1) to falling on the ground and crying, "Abba, Father. . . . Take this cup away from Me; nevertheless, not what I will." In order of time the high priestly "Father, the time has come" precedes the sacrificial "Abba, Father. . . . Not what I will"; but this was only to show beforehand what the intercession would be once the sacrifice was brought. In reality, it was that prayer at the altar in which the prayer before the throne had its origin and its power. Because of the entire surrender of His will in Gethsemane, the High Priest on the throne had the power to ask what He would. He also has the right to let His people share in that power and ask what they will.

The lesson of Gethsemane is one of the most precious and sacred of all. To a superficial learner it may appear to take away the courage to pray in faith. If the earnest supplication of the Son's "Take this cup from Me" was not heard, if He had to say, "Yet not what I will," how much more do we need to say it? It may even appear impossible that the promises the Lord had given only a few hours before—"Whatever you ask"; "Whatever you wish"—could have been meant literally. But a deeper insight into the meaning of Gethsemane teaches us that it is precisely here that we have sure ground and an open way to assurance of an answer to our prayers. He is our Teacher and will open up to us the mystery of His holy sacrifice as revealed in this matchless prayer.

—— *Teach Me to Pray*

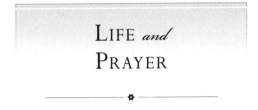

LIFE *and*
PRAYER

---- ✱ ----

They devoted themselves to the apostles' teaching and to the
fellowship, to the breaking of bread and to prayer.

Acts 2:42

Our daily life has tremendous influence on our prayers, just as our prayers influence our daily life. In fact, our life is a continuous prayer. We are continually praising or thanking God by our actions and by the manner in which we treat others. At times God cannot hear the prayer of your lips because the worldly desires of your heart cry out much more loudly and strongly.

As we have said, life exercises a mighty influence over our prayers. A worldly life or a self-seeking life makes prayer by that person powerless and an answer impossible. With many Christians there is conflict between their everyday life and their prayer life, and the everyday life holds the upper hand. But prayer can also exercise a strong influence. If I yield myself completely to God in prayer, prayer can overcome a life in the flesh and the practice of sin. The entire life may be brought under the control of prayer. Prayer can change and renew the life because in prayer we can call upon and receive the Lord Jesus, and ask the Holy Spirit to purify and sanctify us.

Because of what is lacking in their spiritual life, many people think they must make a supreme effort to pray more. They do not understand that only in proportion as the spiritual life is strengthened can the prayer life increase. Prayer and life are inseparably connected and the quality of each deeply related.

How sacred and powerful prayer is when it takes possession of the heart and life! It keeps one constantly in fellowship with God. Then we can literally say, "I wait on you, Lord, all day long." Let us be careful to consider not only the length of time we spend with God in prayer but also the power prayer has over our entire life.

—— *Living a Prayerful Life*

PRAY
WITHOUT CEASING

❖

Pray without ceasing, in everything give thanks; for this is the will
of God in Christ Jesus for you.

1 Thessalonians 5:17–18 NKJV

Who can do this? Does praying without ceasing refer to continual physical acts of prayer in which we persevere until we obtain what we ask, or does it refer to the spirit of prayerfulness that animates and motivates us throughout the day? It includes both. The example of our Lord Jesus shows us this. We should enter our place of private prayer for special seasons of prayer, and at times we are to persevere there in importunate prayer. We are also to walk throughout the day in God's presence, with our whole heart focused on Him. Without set times of prayer, the spirit of prayer will be lacking and weak. Without the continual attitude of prayerfulness, our set times of prayer will be ineffective.

Does this continuous prayer refer only to prayer for ourselves or also for others? It refers to both. The death of Christ took Him to the place of everlasting intercession. Your death with Him to sin and self sets you free from the care of self, elevating you to the dignity of an intercessor—one who can receive life and blessing from God for others. Know your calling; begin your work. Give yourself wholly to it and soon you will find something of this "prayer without ceasing" within you.

Let your faith rest boldly on His finished work. Let your heart wholly identify itself with Him in His death and His life. Like Him, give yourself to God as a sacrifice for others. It is your highest privilege, it is your true and full union with Him; it will be to you, as to Him, your power for intercessory prayer.

—— *The Ministry of Intercessory Prayer*

LIGHT FROM *the* INNER ROOM

❈

Let the hearts of those who seek the Lord rejoice. Look to the Lord and his strength; seek his face always.

1 Chronicles 16:10–11

Think of God, His greatness, His holiness, His unspeakable glory, and then imagine the inestimable privilege to which He invites His children, that each one of them, no matter how sinful or frail, may have access to God at any time and may talk with Him as long as he would like. God is ready to meet His child whenever he enters his prayer room; He is ready to have fellowship with him, to give him the joy and strength that he needs along with the assurance that God is with him and will undertake for him in every situation. In addition, God promises that He will enrich His child's outward life and provide the things he has asked for in secret. We ought to cry out for joy. What an honor! What a salvation!

One might imagine that no place on earth would be as attractive to the child of God as the place of prayer, where the presence of God is promised and unhindered fellowship with the Father awaits. But what is the response? From everywhere the conclusion is reached that private, personal prayer is as a general rule neglected by those who call themselves believers.

Is there no hope of change? The man through whom God has made known the message of the inner room is none other than our Lord Jesus Christ, who saves us from our sins. He is able and willing to deliver us from our lack of prayer and He will deliver us. Even in your sin and your weakness, come into your prayer room and begin to thank God as you have never thanked Him before that the grace of the Lord Jesus makes it possible for you to converse with your Father just as a child ought to.

—— *Living a Prayerful Life*

PRAY *to the* LORD
of the HARVEST

❖

*Then He said to His disciples, "The harvest truly is plentiful but
the laborers are few. Therefore pray the Lord of the harvest to send
out laborers into His harvest."*

Matthew 9:37–38 NKJV

Our Lord frequently taught His disciples that they must pray and how they
should pray, but seldom *what* to pray. This He left to their sense of need and
the leading of the Spirit. But in this text we have one thing He expressly commands them to remember. In view of the abundant harvest and the need of
reapers, he tells them to call on the Lord of the harvest to send forth laborers.
Just as in the parable of the friend who comes at midnight, He wants them
to understand that prayer is not to be selfish. It is the power through which
blessing can come to others. The Father is Lord of the harvest, so when we
pray for the Holy Spirit, we are to pray that He will prepare and send out
laborers for His work.

Is it not strange that He should ask His disciples to pray for this? Could He
not call out laborers? Would not one prayer of His accomplish more than a
thousand of theirs? Did not God, the Lord of the harvest, see the need, and
would He not in His own good time send forth laborers—even without the
disciples' prayers? Such questions lead us to the deepest mysteries of prayer
and its power in the kingdom of God. Answers to such questions convince us
that prayer is indeed a power on which the gathering of the harvest and the
coming of the kingdom truly depend.

Prayer is not meant to be an empty form or show. It calls upon the power
of God. He called on the disciples to pray for laborers to be sent among the
lost because He believed their prayer would accomplish the needed result. The
success of the work would actually depend on them and whether they were
faithful or unfaithful in prayer.

—— *Teach Me to Pray*

MINISTERS
of the SPIRIT

❖

He has made us competent as ministers of a new covenant—not of the letter but of the Spirit; for the letter kills, but the Spirit gives life. . . . If the ministry that condemns men is glorious, how much more glorious is the ministry that brings righteousness!

2 Corinthians 3:6, 9

*M*any pray for the Spirit that they may make use of Him and His power for their work. This is an entirely wrong concept. It is He who must use you. Your relationship toward Him must be one of deep dependence and utter submission.

There are many who think they must only preach the Word and the Spirit will make the Word fruitful. They do not understand that it is the Spirit, in and through the preacher, who will make the Word effective to the heart of the listener. I must not be satisfied with praying that God will bless the Word that I preach through the operation of His Spirit. Rather, the Lord wants me to be filled with the Spirit so that my preaching is a manifestation of the Spirit and power. We see this occurring on the day of Pentecost. They were filled with the Spirit and began to speak through the power of the Spirit who was in them.

When the Lord promised the apostles that they would receive power when the Holy Spirit came upon them, it was as though He said: "Do not preach without this power. It is the indispensable preparation for your work. Everything depends on it."

Every manifestation of the power of the flesh in us and the weakness of our spiritual life must drive us to the conviction that God, through the powerful operation of His Holy Spirit, will work out a new and strong life in us. He will cause the Word to become joy and light in our souls. He will also help us in prayer not only to know the mind and will of God but to find our delight in it.

—— *Living a Prayerful Life*

A LACK *of* PRAYER

❋

No one calls on your name or strives to lay hold of you.

Isaiah 64:7

*W*e all see the contrast between the man whose income barely keeps up his business and maintains his family and the man whose income enables him to expand his business and also help others. There may be an earnest Christian who prays just enough to maintain his position while another prays enough to see further spiritual growth in Christlikeness. The former is more of a defensive attitude, seeking to fight off temptation, rather than an aggressive one that reaches after higher attainment. If we desire to grow from strength to strength and to experience God's power in sanctification and blessing on others, we must be more persevering in prayer.

The law of God is unchangeable; as on earth, so in our communication with heaven, we only get as we give. Unless we are willing to pay the price, to sacrifice our time and attention along with the seemingly legitimate or necessary tasks for the sake of attaining to the spiritual gifts, we need not expect power from above in our work.

God's call to prayer need not be a burden or cause for continual self-condemnation. He intends that it be a joyful task. He can make it a source of inspiration. Through it He can strengthen us in our work and bring blessing to others by His power that works in us.

Without hesitation, let us confess our sin of neglect and confront it in the name of our Mighty Redeemer. *The same light that shows us our sin and condemns us for it will show us the way out of it, into a life of liberty that pleases God.* Let our lack of prayer convict us of the coolness in our Christian life that lies at the root of it. God will use the discovery to bring us not only the power to pray that we long for but also the joy of a new and fruitful life of which prayer is the spontaneous expression.

—— *The Ministry of Intercessory Prayer*

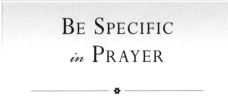

BE SPECIFIC
in PRAYER

❖

"What do you want me to do for you?" Jesus asked him.

Mark 10:51

The blind man had been crying out over and over, "Jesus, Son of David, have mercy on me!" The cry reached the ear of the Lord, who knew what the man wanted, and He was ready to give it to him. But first Jesus asks, "What do you want me to do for you?" He wants to hear from the man's own lips not only the general petition for mercy but also the distinct expression of his desire. Until he declares it, he is not healed.

There are still many to whom the Lord puts the same question and who cannot, until it has been answered, get the help they seek. Our prayers must not be vague appeals to His mercy or indefinite cries for blessing, but the distinct expression of a specific need. It is not that Jesus' loving heart does not understand our cry or is not ready to hear, but He desires that we name our petitions for our own good. Prayer that is intentional teaches us to better know our own desires. To find out what our greatest need is demands time, thought, and self-scrutiny. To find out whether our desires are honest and real, and whether we are ready to persevere in them, we are put to the test. It leads us also to discern whether our desires conform to God's Word and whether we really believe that we will receive the things we ask for. It helps us to wait for a definite answer and to be aware of it when it comes.

To all of us, the Lord asks, "What is it you really want and expect me to do for you?"

—— *Teach Me to Pray*

THE VOICE *of* CONSCIENCE

✿

I speak the truth in Christ—I am not lying, my conscience confirms it in the Holy Spirit.

Romans 9:1

With regard to the knowledge of God's will, we must give conscience its place and submit to its authority. In a thousand little things the law of nature or education teaches us what is right and good, but even earnest Christians do not always feel themselves bound to obey these. If you are unfaithful in that which is least, who will entrust you with greater things? Not God. If the voice of conscience tells you of a course of action that is nobler or better, and you choose something else because it is easier or pleasing to self, you ill-equip yourself for the teaching of the Spirit by disobeying the voice of God. A strong willingness to always do the right thing and to do the very best that conscience dictates is a will to do God's will.

Beware of a legal obedience: striving after a life of true obedience under a sense of duty. Ask God to show you the *newness of life* that is needed for a new and full obedience. Claim this promise: "The Lord your God will circumcise your hearts and the hearts of your descendants, so that you may love him with all your heart and with all your soul, and live" (Deuteronomy 30:6). Believe in the love of God and the grace of our Lord Jesus Christ. Trust the Spirit that is in you, enabling you to love and so cause you to walk in God's statutes. In the strength of this faith, and in the assurance of sufficient grace, which is made perfect in weakness, enter into God's love and the life of living obedience it enables. Nothing but the continual presence of Jesus and His love can prepare you for continual obedience.

—— *A Life of Obedience*

Our Lord's Prayer Life

❋

Very early in the morning, while it was still dark, Jesus got up,
left the house and went off to a solitary place, where he prayed.

Mark 1:35

The connection between the prayer life and the Spirit life is indissoluble. This was evident in the life of our Lord. A study of His life will give us a picture of the power of prayer. While others slept, He went away to pray and to renew His strength in communion with His Father. He needed this time with God—otherwise He would not have been ready for the trials and the blessings of the new day.

Think of the calling of the apostles as recorded in Luke 6:12–13: "One of those days Jesus went out to a mountainside to pray, and spent the night praying to God. When morning came, he called his disciples to him and chose twelve of them." Then one day, "Jesus was praying in a certain place. When he finished, one of his disciples said to him, 'Lord, teach us to pray'" (Luke 11:1). And then He gave them that inexhaustible prayer: "Our Father . . . hallowed be your name. . . ." John 17 records the high-priestly, most holy prayer. It gives us a glimpse into the remarkable relationship between the Father and the Son.

Now look at the most stunning instance of all: In Gethsemane, according to His habit, our Lord consulted and arranged with the Father the work He had to do on earth. First, He besought Him in agony to allow the cup to pass from Him. When He understood that this could not be, He prayed for strength to drink the cup and surrendered himself with the words "Your will be done." He was able to meet the enemy full of courage, and in the power of God gave himself over to death on the cross.

—— *Living a Prayerful Life*

INTERCESSORY PRAYER

❀

Therefore confess your sins to each other and pray for each other so that you may be healed. The prayer of a righteous man is powerful and effective.

James 5:16

James has been speaking of the prayers of the elders of the church; but here he addresses all believers by saying, "Pray for each other so that you may be healed." Having already spoken of confession and of pardon, he still adds, "Confess your sins to each other."

This shows us that the prayer of faith that asks for healing is not the prayer of an isolated believer but of members of the body of Christ united in the Spirit. God certainly hears the prayer of each one of His children as soon as it is presented to Him with living faith, but the one who is sick does not always have this faith, so there must be several members of the body of Christ united in claiming His presence before the Holy Spirit can act with power.

This dependence on the body of Christ should be exercised in two ways: First, we must confess our faults to any whom we may have wronged and receive pardon from them. Apart from this, if the one who is sick sees that a sin he has committed is the cause of his sickness and recognizes his illness as a chastening from God, he ought to acknowledge his sin before the elders or other members of the body of Christ who are able to pray for him with a greater combination of light and faith.

James notes another essential condition to successful prayer: it must be the prayer of the righteous. Whether an elder or layman, it is only after one is wholly surrendered to God and lives in obedience to His will that he can pray effectually for others.

—— *Divine Healing*

THE POWER *of* INTERCESSION

———— ✿ ————

*Therefore I will give him a portion among the great, and he will
divide the spoils with the strong, because he poured out his life
unto death, and was numbered with the transgressors. For he bore
the sin of many, and made intercession for the transgressors.*

Isaiah 53:12

"Tell me where your strength comes from." We might ask this of an intercessor who has had power with God and been successful in prayer. More than one who has desired to give himself to this ministry has wondered why it was so difficult to rejoice in it, to persevere, and to succeed. If we study the lives of the heroes of prayer, we might discover their secrets.

A true intercessor is one whose heart and life are completely given over to God. This is the only condition on which an officer of the court of an earthly ruler could expect to exert much influence. Moses, Elijah, Daniel, and Paul all proved this to be true in the spiritual realm. In fact, our Lord himself proved it, because He did not save us by intercession but by the sacrifice of His own life. His power in intercession was established by His sacrifice; intercession claims what the sacrifice has already won. He first gave himself over to the will of God, winning the power to influence that will. He gave himself for sinners in all-consuming love, earning the power to intercede for them. And there is no other way for us. Wholehearted devotion and obedience to God are the first requirements of an intercessor.

You may say that you don't know how to pray like this and ask how you might be equipped to do so. You feel that you are weak in faith, lacking in love for souls and delight in prayer. The one who would have power in intercession must lay aside these complaints and accept that his nature (in Christ) is perfectly adapted to the work. You are created in Christ to pray; it is your very nature as a child of God to do so.

—— *The Believer's Daily Renewal*

RECOGNIZING *a* LACK *of* PRAYER *in* DAILY LIFE

Who is the Almighty, that we should serve Him? And what profit do we have if we pray to Him?

Job 21:15 NKJV

The holy and most glorious God invites us to come to Him, to converse with Him, to ask Him for the things we need, and to experience the depth of blessing there is in fellowship with Him. He has created us in His own image and has redeemed us by His own Son so that in conversation with Him we should find our greatest delight.

What use do we make of this heavenly privilege? How many of us admit to taking a mere five minutes for prayer! The claim is that there is no time. The reality is that a heart desire for prayer is lacking. Many do not know how to spend half an hour with God. It is not that they absolutely do not pray; they may pray every day—but they have no joy in prayer. Joy is the sign that God is everything to you.

If a friend comes to visit, there is time. We make time—even at the cost of something else—for the sake of enjoying pleasant conversation with our friend. Yes, there is time for everything that truly interests us, but time is scarce to practice fellowship with God and to enjoy being with Him. We find time for someone who can be of service to us; but day after day, month after month passes, and for many there is no time to spend even one hour with God. We must acknowledge that we disrespect and dishonor God when we say we cannot find time for fellowship with Him.

If conscience is to do its work and the contrite heart is to feel its proper remorse, it is necessary for each individual to confess his sins by name. May the Lord lay the burden of the sin of prayerlessness heavy on our hearts if this is something of which we are guilty.

—— *Living a Prayerful Life*

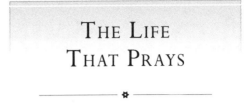

THE LIFE
THAT PRAYS

✿

*If you remain in me and my words remain in you, ask whatever
you wish, and it will be given you.*

John 15:7

*H*ere on earth, the influence of the one who asks a favor for someone else
depends entirely on his character and his relationship with the one to whom
he makes his request. *It is who he is that gives weight to what he asks.* Our power
in prayer depends upon our life. When our life is right, we will know how to
pray so as to please God, and our prayer will secure the answer.

Think for a moment of the people of prayer in Scripture and see in them
what kind of person could pray in such power. We speak of Abraham as an
intercessor. What gave him such boldness? He knew that God had chosen
him and called him away from his home and his people to walk before Him
so that all nations might be blessed through him. He knew that he had obeyed
and forsaken all for God. Implicit obedience, to the very sacrifice of his son,
was the law of his life. He did what God asked so that he dared trust God to
do what he asked.

We pray only as we live. It is our manner of life that enables us to pray. The
life that with wholehearted devotion gives up all *for* God and *to* God can also
claim all *from* God. He waits for hearts that are wholly turned from the world
to Him and that are open to receive His gifts.

The branch that truly abides in Christ, the heavenly Vine, is entirely given up
like Christ to bear fruit unto salvation. Christ's words become part of that one's
life so that he may dare ask whatever he desires—and it will be done for him.

—— *The Ministry of Intercessory Prayer*

56

Preaching Without Prayer Is *in* Vain

❋

Prophesy to these bones and say to them, "Dry bones, hear the word of the Lord!" This is what the Sovereign Lord says to these bones: I will make breath enter you, and you will come to life.

Ezekiel 37:4–5

We are familiar with the vision of the valley of dry bones. There was a noise, and bone came together to bone, and flesh came up, and skin covered them—but there was no breath in them. The prophesying to the bones—the preaching of the Word of God—had a powerful influence. It was the beginning of the great miracle that was about to happen, and there lay an entire army of men newly made. It was the beginning of the work of life in them, but there was no spirit there.

Then he said to me, "Prophesy to the breath; prophesy, son of man, and say to it: 'This is what the Sovereign Lord says: Come from the four winds, O breath, and breathe into these slain, that they may live'" (v. 9). When the prophet had done this, the Spirit came upon them, and they lived and stood on their feet, a very great army. Prophesying to the bones, that is, preaching, has accomplished a great work. But saying to the Spirit: "Come, O Spirit," that is prayer, and that has accomplished a far more wonderful thing. The power of the Spirit was revealed through prayer.

Preaching must always be followed up by prayer. The preacher must come to see that his preaching is powerless to bring new life until he begins to take time for prayer, and according to the teaching of God's Word, he strives and labors and continues in prayer; and he takes no rest and gives God no rest until He bestows the Spirit in overflowing power.

—— *Living a Prayerful Life*

THE FAITH THAT
APPROPRIATES

———— ✿ ————

Therefore I tell you, whatever you ask for in prayer, believe that you have received it, and it will be yours.

Mark 11:24

What a promise—so broad, so divine, that our limited understanding cannot take it in. In every possible way we seek to limit it to what we think safe or probable instead of allowing it to remain as He gave it in all its quickening power and energy. Faith is very far from being a mere conviction of the truth of God's Word or a conclusion drawn from certain premises. It is the ear that has heard God telling what He will do, the eye that has seen Him doing it.

Therefore, where there is true faith, the answer *must* come. If we only do the one thing He asks of us as we pray: "Believe that you have received it," He will do what He has promised: "It *will be yours.*" In this spirit let us listen to the promise Jesus gives; each part of it has its divine message.

"Whatever you ask . . ." When we hear this, our human wisdom begins to doubt and say, "Surely this cannot be literally true." But if it is not, why did the Master say it? "*Whatever* you ask . . ." It is not as if this were the only time He spoke this way. He also said, "*Everything* is possible for him who believes" (Mark 9:23). Faith is so wholly the work of God's Spirit through His Word in the prepared heart of the believing disciple that it is impossible the fulfillment should not come. The tendency of human reasoning is to interpose here certain qualifying clauses—"if expedient"; "if according to God's will"—to break the force of a statement that appears presumptuous. Beware of dealing this way with the Master's words. He wants His Word to penetrate our hearts and reveal how mighty the power of faith is and how our Father places it at the disposal of His children who trust Him.

—— *Teach Me to Pray*

CHRIST
OUR SANCTIFICATION

✿

It is because of him that you are in Christ Jesus, who has become for us wisdom from God—that is, our righteousness, holiness and redemption. Therefore, as it is written: "Let him who boasts boast in the Lord."

1 Corinthians 1:30–31

We need to understand what this life in Christ is and how on our part it may be accepted and maintained. Of this we may be sure, it is not something beyond our reach. There need not be any exhausting effort or hopeless sighing, "Who will ascend into heaven? (that is, to bring Christ down)" (Romans 10:6). This life is meant for the sinful and the weary, for the unworthy and the impotent. It is a life that is the gift of the Father's love and a life that He will reveal in each one who comes in childlike trust to Him. It is a life that is meant for our everyday life. In every varying circumstance and situation this life will make and keep us holy.

Come and yield more fully to God's way of holiness. Let Christ be your sanctification. Not a distant Christ to whom you look but a Christ who is near, all around you, in you. Not a Christ after the flesh, a Christ of the past, but a Christ who is present in the power of the Holy Spirit. Not a Christ whom you can know by your own wisdom, but the Christ of God who is the Spirit within you.

Most blessed Father, I bow in speechless adoration before the holy mystery of your divine love. Forgive me that I have known and believed in your love so much less than it deserves to be known and believed. Accept my praise for what I have seen and tasted of its divine blessedness. Accept, Lord God, the praise of a glad and loving heart that knows it can never praise you enough.

—— *The Path to Holiness*

A Guide to Private Prayer

———— ✿ ————

When you pray, go into your room, close the door and pray to your Father, who is unseen. Then your Father, who sees what is done in secret, will reward you.

Matthew 6:6

As you enter a time of private prayer, let your first focus be to give thanks to God for the unspeakable love that invites you to come to Him and to converse freely with Him.

Prepare yourself for prayer by Bible study. Read a few verses. Take what you readily understand and apply it. Then ask the Father to enlighten all of the passage to your heart and make it applicable.

Now you are ready to turn to serious prayer. Take time to present yourself reverently and in quietness before God. Remember His greatness, holiness, and love. Think over what you want to ask of Him. Never be satisfied with going over the same things every day. Let your prayer be specific, originating either from the Word you have just read or from spiritual needs that you are sensing at the time.

It is easy to make known our personal needs. But we are encouraged to pray for the needs of others as well. Remember your family, your church community and its varied ministries, your neighborhood, and your friends. Enlarge your heart to take up the burden of missions and the church throughout the world. Become an intercessor, and you will experience for the first time the blessedness of being used of God to bless others through prayer.

Do not forget the close bond between the inner room and the outside world. The spirit of prayer should remain with us throughout the day. This attitude is intended to bind us to God, to supply us with power from on high, and to enable us to live for Him alone.

—— *Living a Prayerful Life*

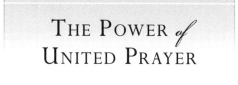

THE POWER *of* UNITED PRAYER

❖

Again I say to you that if two of you agree on earth concerning anything that they ask, it will be done for them by My Father in heaven. For where two or three are gathered together in My name, I am there in the midst of them.

Matthew 18:19–20 NKJV

One of the first lessons our Lord taught about prayer was that our personal prayer time is not to be a spectacle before others. We are to enter an inner room and be alone with the Father. However, He also taught that we need times of public, united prayer as well. He gives a special promise for the gathering of two or three who agree on what they ask.

For its full development, a tree's roots are hidden deep in the ground while its stem or trunk grows upward to the sunlight. In the same way, prayer needs both the private place in which the soul meets God alone and the public fellowship with those who find in the name of Jesus a common meeting place.

The reason for this is quite plain. The bond that unites a Christian to fellow believers is no less real or close than that which unites him to God: he is one with them. Grace renews our relationship not only to God but also with others. Nothing would be more unnatural than for each child of a family to regularly meet with his or her father separately but never in the company of the whole family. Believers are members not only of one family but also of one body. Just as each member of the body depends on the others and the action of the Spirit dwelling in the body depends on the union and cooperation of all, so Christians cannot attain the full blessing God desires to give through His Spirit unless they seek and receive it in fellowship with one another. In the union of believers, the Spirit is free to manifest His full power. It was to the one hundred twenty continuing in one place together and praying with one accord that the Spirit of the glorified Lord came down at Pentecost.

—— *Teach Me to Pray*

CHRIST
OUR INTERCESSOR

--- ✿ ---

*Therefore he is able to save completely those who come to God
through him, because he always lives to intercede for them.*

Hebrews 7:25

Growth in the spiritual life is dependent upon a clear insight into what Jesus is to us. The more we realize that He is *everything* and that all of Christ is for us, the more we will learn to live the true life of faith—dying to self and living completely in Him. The Christian life is not a struggle to live rightly but rather resting in Christ and finding in Him our life and our righteousness. This is especially true in the life of prayer.

Prayer also comes under the law of faith, and when seen in the light of the fullness and completeness that is in Jesus, we will understand that prayer need not be a matter of strain or anxious care but rather an experience of what Christ does through us. It is a participation in the life of Christ, which ascends to the Father as prayer. We can begin to pray not only trusting in the merits of Jesus and in the intercession by which our unworthy prayers are made acceptable, but in that union by which He prays in us and we in Him.

This is illustrated clearly on the last night of Christ's earthly life. In His high-priestly prayer (John 17) He shows us how and what He brings before the Father and what He will pray after His ascension into heaven. His entrance into the work of His eternal intercession *was the beginning and the power of our new prayer life in His name.* A vision of Jesus interceding for us gives us courage to pray in His name.

His people have no need that He conveys in intercession that the Godhead can deny: His mediation on the throne is as real and indispensable as the cross. Nothing takes place without Christ's intercession. It engages all His being and power; it is His unceasing occupation at the right hand of the Father.

—— *Believing Prayer*

SEEKING GOD WITH ALL YOUR HEART

❀

You will seek me and find me when you seek me with all your heart.

Jeremiah 29:13

Experience teaches us that anyone who engages in a task less than wholeheartedly will seldom succeed. Imagine a student, or his teacher, a man of business, or a soldier, who does not give himself to the task at hand. He cannot expect success.

Wholeheartedness is even more essential in spiritual work, and above all, in the high and holy task of prayer and of being well-pleasing to a holy God.

What does your heart tell you? Even though you have given yourself to fulfill your obligations faithfully and zealously, perhaps you need to acknowledge that the reason for an unsatisfactory prayer life is that you have not lived in wholehearted surrender of all that would hinder your fellowship with God.

Prayerlessness is not an isolated thing to be overcome. It is related to the state of the heart. It is a way of life. True prayer depends on an undivided heart. But I cannot give myself an undivided heart, one that enables me to say, "I seek God with my whole heart." In our own strength, it is impossible, but God will do it. He said He would give us a heart to fear Him. He also said He would write His law on our heart. Such promises awaken in us a desire to pray. And if there is a sincere determination to strive after what God has for us, He will work in our heart both to will and to do of His good pleasure. It is the work of the Holy Spirit in us to make us willing. He enables us to seek God with our whole heart.

Let us acknowledge that we have been double-minded, because while we have given ourselves to many earthly things with all our heart, we cannot always say that we have given ourselves to fellowship with God with our whole heart.

—— *Living a Prayerful Life*

ALL THINGS ARE POSSIBLE WITH GOD

---------------------------- ✿ ----------------------------

"Indeed, it is easier for a camel to go through the eye of a needle than for a rich man to enter the kingdom of God." Those who heard this asked, "Who then can be saved?" Jesus replied, "What is impossible with men is possible with God."

Luke 18:25–27

*I*f the great hindrance to the power of God's Spirit working in our lives is our thinking that the standard is an impossible one, we can find hope in these words of Christ, when He tells us that what is impossible with man is possible with God. God can do for us what appears to be beyond our reach. We have this assurance written in His Word that He will do it for us.

In the wondrous union of the divine life and the life of the believer, everything depends on the relationship that is maintained. God must be working and we must be receiving from God through trust and obedience. When this is not understood, we exert our own efforts and take the role that God would fill. We begin to think that if by sincere prayer we can secure God's help, we have found the path to holiness and growth by our efforts. We do not understand that the role of the Spirit must be one of absolute control and our place that of unceasing dependence. This can be seen when two people might be praying that God would give them the Spirit of wisdom or power. One may be thinking only of the limited help that he has always connected with the thought of the Spirit, while the other is expecting that God will do for him above what he could ask or think.

As we think about what God by His Spirit is willing to do in us, we will be convinced that nothing can keep Him from doing His work except something in ourselves. We will understand that our greatest need is to die with Christ to self in order that His life will be our life.

—— *The Believer's Call to Commitment*

A LIFE *of* PRAYER

❋

Be joyful always; pray continually; give thanks in all circumstances.

1 Thessalonians 5:16–18

Our Lord gave the parable of the widow and the unjust judge to teach us that we should always pray and not give up (Luke 18:1–5). Because the widow persevered in seeking one particular thing, the parable seems to refer to persevering in prayer when it appears that God delays or refuses an answer. The words in the Epistles, which speak of continuing in prayer, of watching and praying always in the Spirit, appear to refer more to the whole life being one of prayer. As the soul fills with longing for the manifestation of God's glory and with confidence that He hears the prayers of His children, it rises to full dependence, faith, and trustful expectation.

What is necessary to live such a life of prayer? First, we must sacrifice our life to God's kingdom and for His glory. If we seek to pray without ceasing simply because we want to appear very pious, we will never attain to it. It is by forgetting ourselves and yielding our lives to God that our heart's capacity is enlarged to know God's will. Because everything is weighed and tested by the one thing that fills the heart—the glory of God—and because the soul has learned that only what is of God can honor Him, our whole life becomes one of looking to Him, of crying out from our inmost being for God to prove His power and love and to reveal himself to us.

The believer awakens to the consciousness that he is one of the watchmen on Zion's walls whose call touches and moves the King in heaven to do what would otherwise not be done. To forget oneself and to live for God and His kingdom among men leads to prayer without ceasing.

—— *Teach Me to Pray*

MEDITATION

———— ✾ ————

Blessed is the man who does not walk in the counsel of the wicked or stand in the way of sinners or sit in the seat of mockers. But his delight is in the law of the Lord, and on his law he meditates day and night.

Psalm 1:1–2

Through meditation the heart holds and appropriates the Word of God. Just as in reflection the understanding grasps the meaning and implications of a truth, so in meditation the heart assimilates it and makes it a part of its life. Out of the heart flow the issues of life; whatever the heart truly believes, it embraces with love and joy and thus influences the life. The intellect gathers and prepares the "food" by which we will be nourished. In meditation, the heart digests the food and makes it a part of the life.

The art of meditation needs to be cultivated. A Christian needs to diligently meditate on the Word and consider it until the habit of yielding the whole heart to every word of God is established. The very first requirement is to present ourselves before God. It is *His* Word; it has no power to bless apart from Him. The Word is intended to bring you into His presence and fellowship. Practice His presence and receive the Word as from His hand, confident that He will make it effective in your heart.

The second requirement of true meditation is quiet restfulness. As we study Scripture and try to grasp an argument or master a difficulty, our mind often expends considerable effort. This is not true of meditation. In meditation, we take a truth we have found in the Word or some mystery for which we await divine interpretation and hide it away in the depths of our heart, believing that by the Holy Spirit its meaning and power will be revealed to us. Meditation leads to prayer and by its nature provides subjects for prayer. It motivates us to ask and receive what we have seen in the Word. Meditation is deliberate and wholehearted preparation for prayer.

—— *The Believer's Daily Renewal*

Waiting Patiently
on God

❈

Rest in the Lord, and wait patiently for Him; do not fret because of him who prospers in his way, because of the man who brings wicked schemes to pass. . . . For evildoers shall be cut off; but those who wait on the Lord, they shall inherit the earth.

Psalm 37:7, 9 NKJV

By your patience possess your souls" (Luke 21:19 NKJV). "For you have need of endurance" (Hebrews 10:36 NKJV). "But let patience have its perfect work, that you may be perfect and complete, lacking nothing" (James 1:4 NKJV). Through these words, the Holy Spirit shows us how important patience and endurance are in the Christian life. And nowhere is there a better place for cultivating or displaying it than in waiting on God. There we discover how impatient we are and how our impatience affects our life. We confess at times that we are impatient with others and with circumstances that hinder us or with our slow progress in the Christian life. And if we truly set ourselves to wait on God, we will find that we are impatient with Him because He does not give us what we ask immediately, or as soon as we would like. It is in waiting on God that our eyes are opened to believe in His wise and sovereign will and to see that the sooner and more completely we yield to it, the more surely His blessing will come to us.

Patience honors Him; it allows Him to do His work, yielding self wholly into His hands. It lets God *be God.* If your waiting is for some particular request, wait patiently. If it is the exercise of the spiritual life seeking to know and have more of God, wait patiently. Whether it is in the designated periods of waiting or the continuous habit of the soul, rest in the Lord and be still before Him. You will inherit the land—and all else that God has planned for you.

—— *Waiting on God*

CHRIST ALONE

* ❋ *

Jesus, knowing that they intended to come and make him king by force, withdrew again to a mountain by himself.

John 6:15

The Gospels frequently tell us of Christ's going into solitude for prayer. Luke mentions His praying eleven times. Mark tells us, in his very first chapter, that after an evening of healing many, when all the city had come to see Him, "Very early in the morning, while it was still dark, Jesus got up, left the house and went off to a solitary place, where he prayed" (1:35). Before He chose His twelve apostles, "One of those days Jesus went out to a mountainside to pray, and spent the night praying to God" (Luke 6:12). This idea of complete privacy in prayer appears to have deeply impressed the disciples, giving rise to Mark's remark, "He went up on a mountainside to pray" (6:46); and Matthew's, "He went up on a mountainside by himself to pray. When evening came, he was there alone" (14:23). As a man, Jesus felt the need for absolute solitude.

In the life of a Christian, one of the deepest lessons to learn is that the Word without the living God avails little; that the blessing of the Word comes when it brings us to the living God; that the Word from the mouth of God brings with it the power to understand and to obey it. Let us learn the lesson that personal fellowship with God in secret can make the Word life and power for us.

Prayer allows us to lay our whole life before God and to ask for His teaching and His strength. Attempt for a moment to think what prayer meant to Jesus: It was adoring worship, basking in love, childlike petition for all that He needed. Do we realize what blessedness awaits the one who knows how to follow in Christ's steps? He will prove what great things God can do for the one who makes this his greatest joy—to be alone with Him.

—— *The Believer's Daily Renewal*

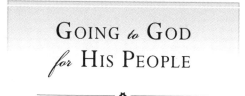

GOING *to* GOD
for HIS PEOPLE

❀

O my God, I trust in You; let me not be ashamed; let not my enemies triumph over me. Indeed, let no one who waits on You be ashamed; let those be ashamed who deal treacherously without cause.

Psalm 25:2–3 NKJV

Think for a moment of the multitudes of people who need that prayer; how many there are who are sick and weary and alone, and who feel that their prayers are not being answered, who sometimes fear that their hope is in vain. Remember, too, the many servants of God, ministers or missionaries, teachers or counselors, whose hope in their work has been disappointed and who long for a manifestation of God's power and blessing. Think of those who have heard of the life of rest and perfect peace, of abiding fellowship with God and His people, of strength and victory, but who cannot find the path to it. In each of these cases there is no explanation but that they have not yet learned the secret of waiting on God. They simply need what we all need: the full assurance that waiting on God is never an exercise in vain.

If this intercession for others becomes a part of our waiting on Him, we will help to bear one another's burdens and so fulfill the law of Christ. There will be introduced into our waiting on God that element of unselfishness and love that is the path to the highest blessing and the fullest communion with God. Christ did not seek to enjoy the Father's love for himself alone; He passed it on to us. So let us also love our neighbor.

Twice in this psalm David speaks of waiting on God for himself; here he thinks of all those who wait on Him. Let this be a reminder to God's children who are weary, or who are going through trials, that there are more people praying for them than they know. Let it move them and us so that in our waiting we can at times forget our own needs and say to the Father: "Answer these who also wait on you."

—— *Waiting on God*

THE BLESSING *of a*
VICTORIOUS PRAYER LIFE

❁

Now to him who is able to do immeasurably more than all we ask or imagine, according to his power that is at work within us, to him be glory in the church and in Christ Jesus throughout all generations.

Ephesians 3:20–21

If we are delivered from the sin of prayerlessness and understand how this deliverance may continue to be experienced, what will be the fruit of our liberty? He who grasps this truth will seek after this freedom with renewed enthusiasm and perseverance. His life and experience will show that he has obtained something of unspeakable worth. He will be a living witness of the blessing found in victory.

Think of the confidence in the Father that will replace the reproach and self-condemnation that characterized our lives before. Think how the hour of prayer may become the happiest time in our whole day, and how God may use us there to share in carrying out His plans, making us a fountain of blessing to the world around us. We can hardly conceive of the power God will bestow when we are freed from the sin of prayerlessness and pray with the boldness that reaches heaven to bring down blessing in the almighty name of Christ.

Prayer is not merely coming to God to ask something of Him. It is, above all, fellowship with God and being brought under the power of His holiness and love.

This does not come to us all at once. God has great patience with His children. As a loving Father He bears with us in our slow progress. Let each child of God rejoice in all that God's Word promises. The stronger our faith, the more earnestly will we persevere to the end.

May God strengthen us to believe that there is certain victory prepared for us and that the blessing will be more than the heart has conceived! God will do this for those who love Him.

—— *Living a Prayerful Life*

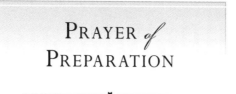

PRAYER *of* PREPARATION

❋

May the grace of the Lord Jesus Christ, and the love of God, and the fellowship of the Holy Spirit be with you all.

2 Corinthians 13:14

Lord God, I thank you that you have led me throughout this week of preparation and that I may now eat with you and your Son on the Lord's Day at the table of your covenant. I thank you for every opportunity for meditation and prayer so that I may not appear carelessly in the sanctuary. In this quiet evening hour, I come once more to ask you for the filling of your Holy Spirit.

You have taught us that without Him there can be no true prayer, no real fellowship. You have given to every one of your children the Holy Spirit, by whom we may have access in Christ to the Father. I ask you that the Spirit might now work in me so as to impart to me the disposition I need to draw near to you together with all your chosen ones. I know that I have sometimes been unfaithful to you. Father, forgive me, and do not take your Holy Spirit from me.

Work in me true penitence so that I may remember my sin with a contrite heart. I desire to remember, confess, and cast away every sin that would cling to me. Let us all here think of our own particular sins and confess them before God in preparation for communion with Him.

I would renounce all confidence in myself and my own good deeds. I want a humble, tender spirit toward you and confidence in your work of grace alone. Then shall my observance of the Supper be truly a fellowship with the Father, Son, and Holy Spirit. Grant this for the sake of your Son. Amen.

—— *The Lord's Table*

THE MINISTRY *of the*
SPIRIT *and* PRAYER

❖

If you then, though you are evil, know how to give good gifts to your children, how much more will your Father in heaven give the Holy Spirit to those who ask him!

Luke 11:13

Christ had just said, "Ask and it will be given to you" (11:9); God's giving is inseparably connected with our asking. He applies this principle especially to the gift of the Holy Spirit. As surely as a father on earth gives bread to his child, so God gives the Holy Spirit to them that ask Him. One great law rules the whole ministry of the Spirit: *We must ask; God must give.* When the Holy Spirit was poured out at Pentecost with a flow that never ceases, it was in answer to prayer.

Of all the gifts of the early church to which we should aspire, there is none more needed than the gift of prayer—prayer that brings the Holy Spirit into the midst of believers. This power is given to those who say, "We will give ourselves to prayer."

Prayer links the King on the throne with the church at His feet. The church, the human link, receives its divine strength from the power of the Holy Spirit, who comes in answer to their prayers. *Where there is much prayer, there will be much of the Spirit; where there is much of the Spirit, there will be ever-increasing prayer.* If prayer was the power by which the early church flourished and triumphed, shouldn't it be the same of the church today?

We have the privilege of offering ourselves to God to labor in prayer for the blessings He has in store for the church. Shouldn't we beseech God to make this truth live in us? And implore Him that we will not rest until we count the practice of intercession our highest privilege? It is the only certain means of obtaining blessing for the church, the world, and our own lives.

—— *The Ministry of Intercessory Prayer*

THE ALL-INCLUSIVE CONDITION *for* ANSWERED PRAYER

❖

If you abide in Me, and My words abide in you, you will ask what you desire, and it shall be done for you.

John 15:7 NKJV

In all God's dealings with us, His promises and their conditions are inseparable. If we fulfill the conditions, He fulfills the promises. What He is to us depends upon what we are willing to be to Him. "Come near to God and he will come near to you" (James 4:8). And so in prayer, the unlimited promise "Ask what you desire" has one simple and natural condition: "If you abide in Me . . ." The Father always hears His Son. God is *in Christ,* and can be reached only because He is in Him. To be *in Him* is our guarantee that our prayers are heard. Fully and wholly *abiding in Him,* we have the right to ask whatsoever we will, and the promise that it will be done is ours as well.

When we compare this promise with the experience of most believers, we are startled by an awesome discrepancy. Who can count the prayers that rise to God without an answer? Either we do not fulfill the condition, or God does not fulfill the promise.

Believers are not willing to admit either, and therefore have devised a way of escape from the dilemma. They add to the promise the qualifying clause our Savior did not put there: If it is God's will . . . That way, they maintain both God's integrity and their own. How sad that they do not accept and hold to the Word as it stands, trusting Christ to vindicate His truth. Then God's Spirit would lead them to see the divine propriety of such a promise to those who truly abide in Christ—in the sense in which He means it—and to confess that failure to fulfill the condition is the sole explanation for unanswered prayer.

—— *Teach Me to Pray*

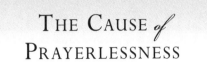

THE CAUSE *of* PRAYERLESSNESS

❋

Those who belong to Christ Jesus have crucified the sinful nature
with its passions and desires. Since we live by the Spirit, let us
keep in step with the Spirit.

Galatians 5:24–25

Scripture teaches us that there are only two conditions possible for the Christian: one is to walk according to the Spirit and the other is to walk according to the flesh. These two powers are in irreconcilable conflict with each other. So most Christians—even though they may be born again through the Spirit and have received the life of God—still continue to live their life according to the flesh and not according to the Spirit.

In Galatians 5, Paul mentions the work of the flesh as not only grave sins such as adultery, murder, and drunkenness, but also the more "ordinary" sins of daily life: anger, strife, and arguing. The majority of Christians have no real knowledge of the deep sinfulness and godlessness of the carnal nature to which they unconsciously yield. The flesh can say prayers well enough, calling itself religious for so doing and thus satisfy the conscience. But the flesh has no desire or strength for the prayer that strives after an intimate knowledge of God, that rejoices in fellowship with Him, and that continues to lay hold of His strength.

The Christian who is still carnal (fleshly) has neither the disposition nor the strength to follow after God. He remains satisfied with his prayer of habit or custom. But the glory and the blessedness of secret prayer is a hidden thing to him, until one day his eyes are opened, and he sees that the flesh in its disposition to turn away from God is the archenemy of powerful prayer.

Do not seek to find in circumstances the explanation for this prayerlessness over which we mourn. Seek it where God's Word declares it to be—in the hidden aversion of the heart to a holy God.

—— *Living a Prayerful Life*

PRAYER *in* HARMONY
WITH *the* PERSON *of* GOD

✿

Father, I thank You that You have heard Me. And I know that You always hear Me, but because of the people who are standing by I said this, that they may believe that You sent Me.

John 11:41–42 NKJV

In the New Testament we find a distinction made between faith and knowledge: "For to one is given the word of wisdom through the Spirit, to another the word of knowledge through the same Spirit, to another faith by the same Spirit, to another gifts of healings by the same Spirit" (1 Corinthians 12:8–9 NKJV). In a child or a childlike Christian there may be faith but little knowledge. Childlike simplicity accepts the truth without difficulty and rarely gives itself or others any reason for its faith except that God said it. But God would have us love and serve Him not only with all our heart but also with our mind so that we might grow up into the divine wisdom and beauty of all His ways and words and works.

This truth has its full application in our prayer life. While prayer and faith are so simple that a newborn convert can pray with power, the doctrine of prayer often presents problems. Is the power of prayer a reality? How can God grant to prayer such power? How can the action of prayer be harmonized with the will of God? How can God's sovereignty and our will, God's liberty and ours, be reconciled? These and other similar questions are valid subjects for Christian meditation and inquiry. The more earnestly and reverently we approach such mysteries, the more we will fall down in adoring awe to praise Him who has given us such power in prayer.

—— *Teach Me to Pray*

THE SECRET *of* EFFECTIVE PRAYER

❋

Therefore I say to you, whatever things you ask when you pray, believe that you receive them, and you will have them.

Mark 11:24

*R*eceiving something from God by faith—believing in the answer with perfect assurance that it has already been given—is not necessarily the experience of the answer or the actual possession of what we have asked for. At times there may be a considerable wait involved. In other cases, the believer may enjoy immediately what he has asked. Of course, in the case of having to wait for the answer, we have a greater need for faith and patience.

We need this faith to be effective intercessors, for grace to pray earnestly and persistently for the lost or needy around us. We must hold fast the divine assurance that as surely as we believe, we will receive. The more we praise God for the answer, the sooner it will be ours.

If you do not immediately see an increase in your desire to pray, do not allow circumstances to hinder or discourage you. Even without any change in feelings, you have accepted the spiritual gift by faith. The Holy Spirit may seem distant, but you may count on Him to pray through you, even if it is only a sigh. In due time, you will again become aware of His full presence and power.

Ask God. Then believe that you have received what you have asked. If you still find it difficult to do this, state your belief on the basis of His Word.

"Believe that you have received." Begin with the faith you have, even if it is weak. Step by step, be faithful in prayer and intercession. The more simply you hold to this truth and expect the Holy Spirit to work, the more surely will this Word become true for you.

—— *The Ministry of Intercessory Prayer*

AMBASSADORS
THROUGH PRAYER

---❖---

Then God said, "Let Us make man in Our image, according to Our likeness." So God created man in His own image; in the image of God He created him; male and female He created them.

Genesis 1:26–27 NKJV

The more we meditate on what prayer is and its power with God, the more we ask, "What is man that you are mindful of him, the son of man that you care for him?" (Psalm 8:4). Sin has so degraded man that from what he is now we can form no concept of what he was meant to be. We must turn back to God's own record of man's creation to discover what God's purpose was and what capacities man was endowed with for that purpose. Man's destiny is clear from God's language at creation. It was to *fill,* to *subdue,* and to *have dominion* over the earth and all that is in it.

When an earthly ruler sends an ambassador to another country, it is understood that he will advise as to the policy to be adopted, and that advice will be acted upon. He is at liberty to apply for troops and any other means needed for carrying out the policy. If his policy is not approved, he is recalled, making way for someone who better understands the ruler's desires. As God's representative, man was to have ruled. On his advice and at his request, heaven was to have bestowed its blessing on earth. His prayer was to have been the channel by which the close relationship between the King in heaven and humankind was to have been maintained. The destinies of the world were given into the power of the wishes, the will, and the prayer of man.

Of course, with the entrance of sin into the picture, this plan underwent a catastrophic change: The fall of man brought all creation under the curse. Only redemption could effect a glorious restoration.

—— *Teach Me to Pray*

STAND AGAINST PRAYERLESSNESS

❖

Let us fix our eyes on Jesus, the author and perfecter of our faith. . . .
Consider him who endured such opposition from sinful men, so that
you will not grow weary and lose heart.

Hebrews 12:2–3

We must not comfort ourselves with thoughts of standing in a right relationship to the Lord Jesus while the sin of prayerlessness has any power over us. But if we first recognize that a right relationship to the Lord Jesus above all else includes prayer, with both the desire and the power to pray according to God's will, then we have reason to rejoice and rest in Him.

Discouragement is the result of self-effort, and so blocks out all hope of improvement or victory. Indeed, this is the condition of many Christians when called on to persevere in prayer as intercessors. They feel it is something entirely beyond their reach. They do not have the power for the self-sacrifice and consecration necessary for such prayer. They have tried in the power of the flesh to conquer the flesh—a wholly impossible thing. They have endeavored, so to speak, to cast out the devil by the devil—and this will never happen. It is Jesus alone who can subdue the flesh and the devil.

We have spoken of a struggle that will certainly result in disappointment and discouragement. This is the effort we make in our own strength. But there is another struggle that will certainly lead to victory. The Scripture speaks of "the good fight of faith" (1 Timothy 6:12), a fight that springs from and is carried on by faith. Jesus Christ is the author and finisher of our faith. When we come into right relationship with Him, we can count on His help and power.

—— *Living a Prayerful Life*

POWER *for* PRAYER *and* WORK

❋

He that believeth on me, the works that I do shall he do also; and greater works than these shall he do; because I go unto my Father. And whatsoever ye shall ask in my name, that will I do, that the Father may be glorified in the Son.

John 14:12–13 KJV

The Savior opened His public ministry to His disciples with the Sermon on the Mount. He closed it by the parting address preserved for us by John. In both messages He spoke more than once of prayer—but with a difference. The Sermon on the Mount was to disciples who had just entered His school, who scarcely knew that God was their Father, and whose prayers' chief reference was to their personal needs. In His closing address, He spoke to disciples whose training time had come to an end, and who were ready as His messengers to take His place and do His work.

In the former, the primary lesson is to be childlike, to pray in faith, and to trust the Father to give good gifts. Now He points to something higher. Now they are His friends to whom He has made known all He has heard from His Father. They are His messengers who have entered into His plans and into whose hands the care of His work and kingdom on earth is to be entrusted. They are to go out and do His work, and in the power of His approaching exaltation, even greater works. Prayer is to be the channel through which that power is received for their work. With Christ's ascension to the Father, a new epoch begins, both for their work and for their life of prayer.

He who would work *must pray.* In prayer, power for your work is obtained. As long as Jesus was here on earth, He did the greatest works. The same demons that the disciples could not cast out fled at His word. When Jesus went to the Father, He was no longer here in body to do the work. The disciples became His body. All His work from the throne must and could be done through them. And now it is done through us.

—— *Teach Me to Pray*

WAITING *in* HOLY EXPECTATION

---------------- ❄ ----------------

Therefore I will look to the Lord; I will wait for the God of my salvation; my God will hear me.

Micah 7:7 NKJV

A book I read some time ago contained one of the best sermons I have seen on the text of this chapter. It told of a king who prepared a city for some of his poor subjects. Not far from their homes were large storehouses where everything they could possibly need was supplied if they would just send in their requests. There was only one condition: They must be on the lookout to receive the answer to their request so that when the king's messengers came with supplies, they would always be found waiting and ready to receive them. The sad story goes on to tell of one despondent subject who never expected to get what he asked for because he felt too unworthy. One day he was taken to the king's storehouses, and there to his amazement he saw all the packages addressed to him. Deliveries had been attempted, but the packages always came back. There was the garment of praise, and the oil of joy, and the eye salve he had asked for, and so much more. The messengers had been to his door, but always found it closed and no one around to receive the packages.

When we have made special requests to God, our waiting must involve the confidence that God hears us. Holy, joyful expectancy is the very essence of true waiting. It is important to remember that it is *God* who works in us. For this to happen, our efforts must cease. Our hope must be in the work of God who raised Jesus from the dead. More than ever, our waiting must become a lingering before God in stillness of soul, depending on Him who raises the dead and calls the things that are not as though they were.

Every moment of a life in the will of God must be of His working. I have only to look to Him, to wait for Him, and to know that He hears me.

—— *Waiting on God*

PERSEVERING
PRAYER

❖

*And he spake a parable unto them to this end, that men ought
always to pray, and not to faint. . . . And shall not God avenge his
own elect, which cry day and night unto him, though he bear long
with them? I tell you that he will avenge them speedily. Nevertheless
when the Son of man cometh, shall he find faith on the earth?*

Luke 18:1, 7–8 KJV

The necessity of praying with perseverance is the secret of all spiritual life. What a blessing to be able to ask the Lord for grace until He gives it, knowing with certainty that it is His will to answer prayer! But what a mystery for us is the call to persevere in prayer, to remind Him of His promises, and to do so without growing weary, until He arises and grants us our petition.

More than once the Bible explains to us the need for persevering prayer. There are many grounds, the chief of which is the justice of God. God has declared that sin must bear its consequences; sin has rights over a world that welcomes and remains enslaved by it (See Romans 6:16). When the child of God seeks to quit this order of things, it is necessary that the justice of God should consent to this. Time, therefore, is needed for the privileges that Christ has procured for believers to be weighed before God's judgment seat. Another reason is the opposition of Satan, who always seeks to prevent the answer to prayer. The only means by which this unseen enemy can be conquered is through faith.

Finally, perseverance in prayer is necessary for us. Delay in the answer is intended to prove and strengthen our faith; it ought to develop in us the steadfast will that no longer lets go of the promises of God but that renounces its own side of things to trust in God alone. It is then that God, seeing our faith, finds us ready to receive His favor and grants it to us. And even though there may be delays, He will not make us wait a moment too long. If we cry unto Him day and night, in due time He will answer.

—— *Divine Healing*

THE HOLINESS
of GOD

--- ✿ ---

But just as he who called you is holy, so be holy in all you do;
for it is written: "Be holy, because I am holy."

1 Peter 1:15–16

It has often been said that the church has lost the concept of sin and the holiness of God. In the secret place of prayer we may learn anew how to give God's holiness the place it should have in our faith and our life. Nowhere can we get to know the holiness of God and come under its influence and power except in private prayer. It has been well said: "No one can expect to make progress in holiness who is not often and long alone with God."

If we remain without any practice of prayer, we make it impossible for God to impart His holiness to us. Let us ask God to forgive us if we have slacked off in this discipline, and to draw us close to himself by His grace and mercy, enabling us to have fellowship with Him who is holy.

The meaning of the words *the holiness of God* is not easily expressed. But we may begin by saying that they imply the unspeakable aversion and hatred with which God regards sin. If you want to understand what that means, remember that He preferred to see His Son die than that sin should reign in us. Think of the Son of God, who gave up His life rather than act in the smallest matter against the will of the Father. He had such a hatred of sin that He chose to die rather than let men be held in its power. That is a portion of the holiness of God. It is a pledge that He will do anything for us in order to deliver us from sin.

Do not think lightly of that grace. You have a holy God who longs to make you holy. Obey the voice of God that calls you to spend time with Him in the stillness of your prayer room so that He may cause His holiness to rest on you.

—— *Living a Prayerful Life*

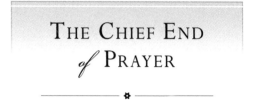

THE CHIEF END
of PRAYER

❖

"Father, glorify your name!" Then a voice came from heaven,
"I have glorified it, and will glorify it again."

John 12:28

or this reason Jesus on His throne in glory will do whatever we ask in His name. Every answer to prayer He gives will have this as its object: When there is no prospect of the Father being glorified, He will not answer. As it was with Jesus, our motivation in prayer must be the glory of the Father—the aim, the end, the very soul and life of our prayers.

Jesus said that nothing glorifies the Father more than His doing what we ask. He will not pass up an opportunity to answer our prayers if we make His goals our goals. The glory of the Father is the link between our asking and His doing. Such prayer cannot fail to be heard and answered.

It is not that we do not at times pray with that motive, but we grieve that we seldom do. And we know the reason for our failure: The gulf between the spirit of daily life and the spirit of prayer is too great. We begin to see that the desire for the glory of the Father is not something that we can stir up and present to our Lord only when we prepare to pray. It is when our whole life is surrendered to God's glory that we can truly pray with that motive.

When our prayers cannot be answered, the Father is not glorified. We must live and pray so that our prayers can be answered and so glorify God. Let us learn how to pray aright for the sake of God's glory.

—— *Teach Me to Pray*

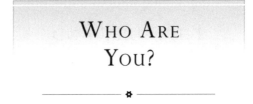

WHO ARE YOU?

❖

Set your minds on things above, not on earthly things. For you died, and your life is now hidden with Christ in God.

Colossians 3:2–3

Upon entering God's presence in the morning hour, a great deal depends upon our realizing not only who *God* is but who we are and what our relationship is to Him. The question: *Who are you?* is asked (not in words but in spirit) of each one who claims right of access and an audience with the Most High. We must have an answer in our inmost consciousness; and that consciousness must be a living sense of the place we have in Christ before God. The mode of expressing it may differ at various times, but in substance it will always be the same.

Who am I? Let me think about that and not be afraid to tell God who it is that shall meet with Him and spend the day. I know, by the Word and Spirit of God, that I am in Christ and that my life is hidden with Christ in God. In Christ I died to sin and the world. By His Spirit, I am taken out of them, separated from them, and delivered from their power. I have been raised together with Christ and in Him I live unto God. Because my life is hidden with Christ, I come to God to claim and obtain the divine life that is hidden in Him for my needs this day.

"Yes, this is who I am," I say to God in humble, holy reverence. Seek and expect nothing less than grace to live here on earth the blessed life of heaven. I can say with confidence, "Christ is my life." The longing of my soul is for Christ to be revealed by the Father within my heart. Nothing less can satisfy me. My life dwells with Christ in God. He can be my life in no other way than as He is in my heart. I can be content with nothing less than Christ in me—Christ as my Savior from sin, Christ as the gift and bestower of God's love, Christ as my indwelling Friend and Lord.

—— *The Believer's Daily Renewal*

THE HOLY SPIRIT IS *the* SPIRIT *of* PRAYER

❋

Because you are sons, God sent the Spirit of his Son into our hearts, the Spirit who calls out, "Abba, Father."

Galatians 4:6

Is it not unfortunate that our thoughts about the Holy Spirit are so often coupled with grief and self-reproach? Yet He bears the name of Comforter, or Counselor, and is given to lead us to find in Christ our highest delight and joy. God grant that our meditation on the work of the Holy Spirit may cause rejoicing and the strengthening of our faith.

The Holy Spirit is the Spirit of prayer. He is called in Zechariah 12:10 "a spirit of grace and supplication." In Romans there is a remarkable reference to Him in the matter of prayer: "For you did not receive a spirit that makes you a slave again to fear, but you received the Spirit of sonship. And by him we cry, 'Abba, Father'" (Romans 8:15).

Have you ever meditated on the words *Abba, Father*? By that address our Savior offered His greatest prayer to the Father, accompanied by the total surrender and sacrifice of His life and love. The Holy Spirit is given for the express purpose of teaching us from the very beginning of our Christian life to address God with those words in childlike trust and surrender.

The Christian left on his own does not know how to pray or for what he ought to pray. But God has stooped to meet us in this weakness by giving us the Holy Spirit to pray through us. The intervention of His Spirit in prayer is deeper than our thoughts or feelings, but is acknowledged and answered by God.

Think of it! In every prayer the triune God takes a part—the Father who hears, the Son in whose name we pray, and the Spirit who prays for us and in us. How important it is that we are in right relationship to the Holy Spirit and that we understand His work.

—— *Living a Prayerful Life*

THE INTERVENTION
of the SPIRIT

❂

Likewise the Spirit also helps in our weaknesses. For we do not know what we should pray for as we ought, but the Spirit Himself makes intercession for us with groanings which cannot be uttered. Now He who searches the hearts knows what the mind of the Spirit is, because He makes intercession for the saints according to the will of God.

Romans 8:26–27 NKJV

*O*f all the offices of the Holy Spirit, the one that leads us most deeply into the understanding of His place in the divine economy of grace is the work He does as the Spirit of prayer. We have the Father *to* whom we pray and who hears our prayer. We have the Son *through* whom we pray and through whom we receive and appropriate the answer because of our union with Him. And we have the Holy Spirit, *in* whom we pray, and who prays through us according to the will of God with such deep, unutterable sighing that God has to search the hearts to know what is the mind of the Spirit.

Just as wonderful and real as the work of God on His throne is the work of the Holy Spirit in us in the prayer that waits and obtains an answer. The intercession within is as divine as the intercession above.

What the Father has purposed and the Son has procured can be appropriated and take effect in the body of Christ only through the continual intervention and active operation of the Holy Spirit. This is especially true of intercessory prayer. The coming of the kingdom, the increase of grace, knowledge, and holiness in believers, their growing devotion to God's work, the effectual working of God's power on the unconverted through the means of grace, all await us from God through Christ. The Holy Spirit has been assigned the task of preparing the body of Christ to reach out, receive, and hold on to what has been provided.

—— *The Indwelling Spirit*

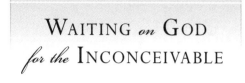

WAITING *on* GOD *for the* INCONCEIVABLE

❖

For since the beginning of the world men have not heard nor perceived by the ear, nor has the eye seen any God besides You, who acts for the one who waits for Him.

Isaiah 64:4 NKJV

Our text emphasizes how God *acts* on behalf of those who wait on Him. The King James Version speaks of *what* God has prepared for us. Our responsibility is to wait on God. What will then be revealed is beyond what the human heart can conceive. Whether it is *what* He has prepared or what He will *do* for us—either is more than we who are finite beings should expect from an Almighty God. But He wants us to expect it. He wants us to believe and trust Him for what to us is impossible.

The previous verses to our text refer to the low state of God's people. The prayer has been poured out: "Look down from heaven, and see" (63:15). "Why have You . . . hardened our heart from Your fear? Return for Your servants' sake" (v. 17). And 64:1–2 is still more urgent, "Oh, that You would rend the heavens! That You would come down! That the mountains might shake at Your presence—as fire burns brushwood, as fire causes water to boil—to make Your name known to Your adversaries, that the nations may tremble at Your presence!"

The need of God's people, and the call for God's mediation, is as urgent in our day as it was then. Nothing but a special outpouring of almighty power will accomplish what is needed. We must desire and believe; we must ask and expect that God will do what is inconceivable to our finite minds. The miracle-working God who surpasses all our expectations must be the God of our confidence.

May we enlarge our hearts to wait on God, who is able to do much more than we could ask or think.

—— *Waiting on God*

THE HOLY TRINITY
MANIFESTED *on the* EARTH

❖

May the grace of the Lord Jesus Christ, and the love of God [the Father],
and the fellowship of the Holy Spirit be with you all.

2 Corinthians 13:14

God is an ever-flowing fountain of pure love and blessedness. Christ is the reservoir wherein the fullness of God was made visible as grace, and has been opened for us. The Holy Spirit is the stream of living water that flows from under the throne of God and of the Lamb.

God's believing children, the Redeemed, are the channels through which the love of the Father, the grace of Christ, and the powerful operation of the Spirit are manifested on earth and imparted to others.

What a clear picture we get here of the wonderful partnership in which God includes us as dispensers of the grace of God! The time we spend in prayer covering our own needs is only the beginning of the true life of prayer. The glory of prayer is that we have power as intercessors to bring the grace of Christ and the energizing power of the Spirit upon those that are still in darkness. The more we yield ourselves to fellowship with the triune God, the sooner we will gain the courage and power to intercede for others.

The more closely the channel is connected with the reservoir, the more certainly will the water flow unhindered through it. The more we are occupied in prayer with the fullness of Christ and the Spirit who proceeds from Him, the more firmly will we abide in fellowship with Him and the more surely will our lives be full of His joy and strength. Are we channels that remain open so that the living water may flow through to the thirsty souls in a dry and barren land?

God is an ever-flowing fountain of love and blessing, and I, as His child, am a living channel through which the Spirit and His life can flow on the earth every day.

—— *Living a Prayerful Life*

HEAVENLY KEEPING

✿

Praise be to the God and Father of our Lord Jesus Christ! In his great mercy he has given us new birth into a living hope through the resurrection of Jesus Christ from the dead, and into an inheritance that can never perish, spoil or fade . . . kept in heaven for you, who through faith are shielded by God's power.

1 Peter 1:3–5

Are you willing to fully experience the heavenly keeping for the heavenly inheritance? Scottish minister Robert Murray M'Cheyne (1813–1843) said, "O God, make me as holy as a pardoned sinner can be made." And if you will pray that earnestly, from the depths of your heart, come and enter into a covenant with the everlasting and omnipotent Jehovah, and in your helplessness, but in restfulness, place yourself into His hands. And then as you enter into that covenant, take with you the promise that the everlasting God will be your companion. The keeper of our souls is watching over us; our Father delights to reveal himself to us. He has the power to let the sunshine of His love guide us throughout the day.

Do not be afraid that because you have a job not directly related to God's work, you cannot have God always with you. Learn a lesson from the natural sun that shines upon us all through the day; wherever we are, we each receive the blessing of its light and warmth. And God will see that His divine light shines upon you and that you abide in that light. He can use you wherever you are.

There is God's omnipotence and our faith reaching out to it. Can we say, "Father, I am going to trust you for your keeping power"? Are not the two sides of this heavenly life wonderful? God's omnipotence covers me, and my small will rests in that power and rejoices in it!

—— *Absolute Surrender*

THE ARMOR *of* GOD
and the SPIRIT *of* PRAYER

❀

Take the helmet of salvation, and the sword of the Spirit, which is
the word of God; praying always with all prayer and supplication
in the Spirit, being watchful to this end with all perseverance and
supplication for all the saints—and for me, that utterance may
be given to me, that I may open my mouth boldly to make known
the mystery of the gospel, for which I am an ambassador in chains;
that in it I may speak boldly, as I ought to speak.

Ephesians 6:17–20 NKJV

hese words are connected with the preceding context: "Be strong in the
Lord. . . . Put on the whole armor of God" (6:10–11). Our battle is against the
spiritual hosts of wickedness in heavenly places. We are to put on the whole
armor of God, both defensive and offensive, with prayer and supplication,
praying at all times in the Spirit. This is done in total dependence upon God.

A life of prayer is the secret of a life of victory. Praying in the Spirit is the
mark of a normal Christian life. Just as my lungs continuously take in air and
my heart continues to beat to sustain my physical life, the Holy Spirit breathes
in me the prayers through which the powers of the divine life are maintained.
Salvation is not won by our own works or our own efforts. It is the gift of God
to us through His Son. I am God's workmanship, created in Christ Jesus *for*
good works that God declares are already prepared for me to walk in. Unceasing prayer is possible, even commanded, because the eternal Spirit maintains
it as the spiritual breathing of the soul.

Praying at all times is never to be selfish in nature, remembering only our
own needs. Paul speaks in our text of the unity of the saints forming one great
army of the Lord, living by one Spirit and striving together for the establishment
of His kingdom in the world. Continual prayer is not only the responsibility
of each member, but the essential factor upon which the whole body depends.

—— *The Believer's Call to Commitment*

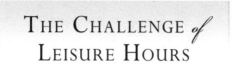

THE CHALLENGE *of* LEISURE HOURS

❖

If the owner of the house had known at what hour the thief was coming, he would not have let his house be broken into.

Luke 12:39

It is in the leisure hours, when we are free from constraint and observation, that we are more apt to reveal what is truly important to us. In the spiritual life this is true as well. While in college, for instance, the mind of a student is inclined toward systematic work so that his time for prayer or Bible study is often kept as regularly as his classes or individual study. When extended periods of leisure occur, and we are free to do as we wish, we find that Bible study and fellowship with God in prayer do not come so naturally. And so times of leisure become a test of character, the proof as to whether one could say with Job, "I have treasured the words of his mouth more than my daily bread" (23:12). The relaxation of regular habits and the subtle thought that we are at liberty to do as we please set many a person back in his Christian life.

The progress of months may be lost by the neglect of one week. We do not know at what hour the thief will come. Just as we need during leisure hours to eat regular meals and breathe fresh air, so we need to daily eat the bread of life and breathe the air of heaven. The morning devotional hour is not only a duty but an unspeakable privilege and pleasure. Fellowship with God—abiding in Christ, loving His Word and meditating on it throughout the day—is life and strength to the Christian, health and gladness to the new nature.

God has created and redeemed us so that through us He may—as the sun illuminates the world—shine His light and life and love upon the people around us. In order to do this, we need to be in daily communication with the fountain of light.

—— *The Believer's Daily Renewal*

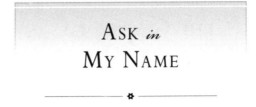

ASK *in*
MY NAME

❖

In that day you will no longer ask me anything. I tell you the truth,
my Father will give you whatever you ask in my name. Until now
you have not asked for anything in my name. Ask and you will
receive, and your joy will be complete.

John 16:23–24

To understand how the coming of the Holy Spirit was indeed to begin a new epoch in the prayer world, we must remember who He is, what His work is, and the significance of His not being given until Jesus was glorified. It is in the Spirit that God exists, for He is Spirit. It is in the Spirit that the Son was begotten of the Father. It is in the fellowship of the Spirit that the Father and the Son are one. The eternal, never-ending giving to the Son that is the Father's prerogative, and the eternal asking and receiving that is the Son's right and authority—it is through the Spirit that this communion of life and love is maintained. It has been so from all eternity. It is especially so now, when the Son as Mediator ever lives to pray for us.

The work that Jesus began on earth, of reconciling in His own body both God and man, is now carried on in heaven. To accomplish this, He took up in His own person the conflict between God's righteousness and our sin. In His body on the cross He once for all ended the struggle. Then He ascended to heaven so that from there He might in each member of His body carry out the deliverance and manifest the victory He had obtained. To do this, He ever lives to pray, and in His unceasing intercession, He places himself in living fellowship through the prayer of His redeemed ones. It is His intercession that shows itself in our prayers and gives them power that they never had before. All this is done through the Holy Spirit.

—— *Teach Me to Pray*

THE HOLY SPIRIT *and* OUR HOLINESS

✿

From the beginning God chose you to be saved through the sanctify-ing work of the Spirit and through belief in the truth.

2 Thessalonians 2:13

The name *Holy Spirit* teaches us that it is particularly the work of the Spirit to impart holiness to us and make it our own.

The holiness of God in Christ becomes holiness in you because His Spirit dwells in you. The words *Holy* and *Spirit* and the divine realities they represent are now inseparably and eternally united. *You can only have as much of the Spirit as you are willing to have of holiness.* And you can only have as much holiness as you have the indwelling Spirit.

Some pray for the Spirit because they long to have His light and joy and strength, but their prayers accomplish little increase of His blessing or power. It is because they do not truly know or desire Him as the *Holy* Spirit. They are not acquainted with His burning purity, His convicting light, His putting to death the deeds of the flesh, and His leading into the fellowship of Jesus, who gave up His will and His life to the Father.

He reveals and imparts the holiness of Christ. Jesus speaks of "the Holy Spirit, whom the Father will send in my name, [who] will teach you all things and will remind you of everything I have said to you" (John 14:26). He is the Spirit of Christ. Our hope is awakened to believe that He will work mightily in us.

"Whoever believes in me . . . streams of living water will flow from within him" (John 7:38). Be assured that the Spirit, who is already within us, will do His work in ever-increasing power.

—— *The Path to Holiness*

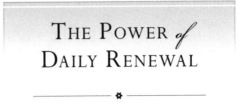

THE POWER *of* DAILY RENEWAL

---- ✿ ----

*Though outwardly we are wasting away, yet inwardly we are being
renewed day by day.*

2 Corinthians 4:16

Every day our natural life is renewed. The sun rises with its light and warmth, the flowers open, the birds sing, and life is everywhere stirred and strengthened. As we rise from a night's sleep and refresh ourselves with food, we feel we have gathered new strength for the duties of the day. Awareness of our need for prayer and reading the Word each day is the confession that our inward life needs daily renewal, too. Only by fresh nourishment from God's Word and fresh communion with God himself in prayer can the vitality of the spiritual life be maintained and grow. Just as our bodies need rest and nourishment for daily life as well as for times of sickness, stress of work, and fatigue, so the inward man must be renewed daily.

Even our time of quiet and prayer and study of the Word is only effective when the Spirit of God works through them. Our study would be lacking if we did not emphasize the daily renewal of the inward person, which the Spirit himself performs. In Romans 12:2 we read of the progressive transformation of the Christian life that comes by "the renewing of [the] mind." In Ephesians 4:22–23, the phrase *"to put off your old self"* indicates an act done once for all, but the words *"be transformed by the renewing of your mind"* are in the present tense and indicate a progressive work. It says in Colossians 3:10: "Put on the new self, which is being renewed in knowledge in the image of its Creator." We are to look to the blessed Spirit on whom we can count for daily renewal of the inner person in the place of prayer.

—— *The Believer's Daily Renewal*

A Manifestation *of* God's Power

✿

"Now, Lord, consider their threats and enable your servants to speak your word with great boldness. Stretch out your hand to heal and perform miraculous signs and wonders through the name of your holy servant Jesus." After they prayed, the place where they were meeting was shaken. And they were all filled with the Holy Spirit and spoke the word of God boldly.

Acts 4:29–31

*I*s it permissible to pray in this way, to ask the Lord to enable His servants to speak His Word with great boldness and to stretch out His hand to heal?

The Word of God encounters as many difficulties in our day as it did then, and the needs today are equally pressing. Imagine the apostles in the midst of Jerusalem: On the one hand, there were the rulers of the people with their threatenings; on the other, the blind multitude refusing to believe in the crucified Christ. The world today may not be so openly hostile to the church because it has lost its fear of her, but its flattering words are more to be dreaded than its hatred. Dissimulation is sometimes worse than violence. The help of God is as necessary now as it was then. The apostles well knew that it was not the eloquence of their preaching that caused the truth to triumph but the manifest presence of the Holy Spirit through miracles. It was necessary that the living God stretch forth His hand in healings, miracles, and signs in the name of Jesus. It was then that His servants rejoiced and were strengthened by His presence. They felt freedom to speak His Word with boldness and to teach the world to fear His name.

The divine promises are also for us. It is nowhere found in the Bible that this promise was not for future times. In all ages God's people need to know that the Lord is with them and to possess the irrefutable proof of it. The promise is for us; let us pray for its fulfillment.

—— *Divine Healing*

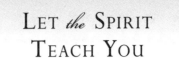

LET *the* SPIRIT
TEACH YOU

❋

Who is it that overcomes the world? Only he who believes that
Jesus is the Son of God. This is the one who came by water and
blood—Jesus Christ. . . . And it is the Spirit who testifies, because
the Spirit is the truth.

1 John 5:5–6

Do you ever wonder why there are not more men and women who can witness with joyful hearts that the Spirit of God has taken possession of their lives and given them new power to witness? What is it that hinders us? The Father in heaven is more willing than an earthly father to give bread to his child, and yet the cry arises "Is the Spirit restricted or hampered? Is this His work?"

Some will acknowledge that the hindrance undoubtedly lies in the fact that the church is under the sway of the flesh and the world. They understand too little of the heart-changing power of the cross of Christ. Because of this, the Spirit does not have vessels into which He can pour His fullness.

But I bring you a message of joy. The Spirit who is in you, in however limited a measure, is prepared to bring you under His teaching, to lead you to the cross, and by His heavenly instruction to make you aware of what the crucified Christ wants to do for you and in you.

He will show you how the neglect of private prayer has hindered your fellowship with Christ; He will reveal the cross to you and the powerful operation of the Spirit. He will teach you what is meant by self-denial, taking up your cross daily, and losing your life in order to follow Him.

In spite of your having acknowledged your ignorance, your lack of spiritual insight and fellowship with the cross, He is willing to teach you and to make known to you the secret of a spiritual life beyond all your expectations.

—— *Living a Prayerful Life*

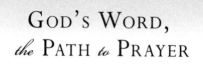

GOD'S WORD,
the PATH *to* PRAYER

❖

I am the vine; you are the branches. If a man remains in me and I
in him, he will bear much fruit; apart from me you can do nothing.

John 15:5

God's Word prepares us for prayer by revealing what the Father would have us ask. And it is God's Word that strengthens us in prayer by giving our faith the grounds for asking. After we have prayed, it is God's Word that brings the answer, for through it the Spirit shows us that we have heard the Father's voice.

Prayer should not be a monologue but a dialogue; God's voice in response to mine is its most essential part. Listening to God's voice is the secret of the assurance that He will listen to mine. What God's words are to me is the test of what He is to me and also of the sincerity of my desire after Him in prayer.

Jesus points to this connection between His Word and our prayer when He says, "I am the vine; you are the branches. If a man remains in me and I in him, he will bear much fruit; apart from me you can do nothing."

God gives us himself through His Word. His Word is nothing less than the eternal Son, Jesus Christ. All the words of Christ are God's words, full of divine life and power. "It is the Spirit who gives life; the flesh profits nothing. The words that I speak to you are spirit, and they are life" (John 6:63 NKJV).

To pray, or give utterance to certain wishes and appeal to certain promises, is an easy thing, and can be learned by anyone through human wisdom. But to pray in the Spirit and speak words that reach and touch God, that affect and influence the powers of the unseen world—such praying and speaking depend entirely upon our hearing God's voice.

—— *Teach Me to Pray*

Waiting *on* God *to* Supply

———— ✿ ————

The Lord upholds all who fall, and raises up all who are bowed down. The eyes of all look expectantly to You, and You give them their food in due season.

Psalm 145:14–15 NKJV

*I*f an army has been sent out to march into enemy territory and news is received that it is not advancing, the question is immediately asked, "What is the cause of the delay?" The answer will very often be, "We are waiting for supplies." If provisions of gear or ammunition have not arrived, they dare not proceed. So it is in the Christian life: Day by day we need supplies from above. And there is nothing more necessary than cultivating a spirit of dependence on God and of confidence in Him that refuses to go on without the needed supply of grace and strength.

It is especially at the time of prayer that we ought to cultivate this spirit of quiet waiting. Before you pray, bow quietly before God; remember and realize who He is, how near He is, how certainly He can and will help. Be still before Him and allow His Holy Spirit to awaken in your soul the childlike disposition of absolute dependence and confident expectation. Wait on God as you would a living person. He is the living God who is aware of you and is longing to fulfill all of your needs. Wait on God until you know you have met with Him. Your prayer time will never be the same.

Waiting on Him will become the most blessed part of prayer, and the answer to your prayer will be all the more precious because it is the fruit of fellowship with Him.

God provides in nature for the creatures He has made. How much more will He provide in grace for those He has redeemed! Learn to say about every want, failure, or lack of the grace you need, I have not waited enough on God. He would have given me all I needed in due season.

—— *Waiting on God*

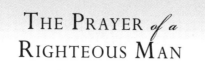

THE PRAYER *of a* RIGHTEOUS MAN

❋

Therefore confess your sins to each other and pray for each other so that you may be healed. The prayer of a righteous man is powerful and effective. Elijah was a man just like us. He prayed earnestly that it would not rain, and it did not rain on the land for three and a half years. Again he prayed, and the heavens gave rain, and the earth produced its crops.

James 5:16–18

James knew that a faith that obtains healing is not the fruit of human nature; therefore he adds the word *powerful* to the description of the prayer of a righteous man. Only such prayer can be effective. In this he stands on the example of Elijah, a man "just like us," drawing the inference that our prayer can be and ought to be of the same nature as his. How did Elijah pray?

Elijah had received from God the promise that rain was about to fall upon the earth and he had declared this to Ahab. Strong in the promise of his God, he ascended Mount Carmel to pray (1 Kings 18:42). He knew that it was God's will to send rain, but he also knew he needed to pray or the rain would not come.

This is how prayer is to be made for the sick. The promise of God must be relied on and His will to heal recognized. After the prayer of faith comes the prayer of perseverance, which does not lose sight of what has been asked until God has fulfilled His promise. It might seem strange to us that after having prayed with the certainty of being heard and seeing in it the will of God, we should still need to pray. In Gethsemane, Jesus prayed three times in succession. On Mount Carmel Elijah prayed seven times; and we, if we believe the promise of God without doubting, shall pray until we receive the answer. If we learn to persevere in prayer, we will obtain the healing of the sick, just as Jesus did when He was on earth—a miraculous healing that glorifies God.

—— *Divine Healing*

LIFTED INTO
GOD'S PRESENCE

———————— ✿ ————————

Oh, how I love your law! I meditate on it all day long. . . . See how I love your precepts; preserve my life, O Lord, according to your love. . . . I obey your statutes, for I love them greatly.

Psalm 119:97, 159, 167

*O*ne portion of Scripture that is wholly devoted to teaching us the place God's Word ought to have in our lives is Psalm 119. It is the longest chapter in the Bible, and almost without exception every one of its 176 verses mentions the Word of God under various names. Those who would like to know how to study the Bible according to God's will ought to make a careful study of Psalm 119. We cannot wonder why our Bible study does not benefit us more if we neglect the direction of this Psalm. Maybe you have never read it through as a whole. You would be wise to find the time to read it through, absorb its theme, or at least catch its spirit. If you find it difficult to do this by reading it once, read it more than once. This will help you to see the need of giving it more careful thought.

The Word of God becomes a rich and inexhaustible basis for holding communion with God. As we gradually gain insight into its truths, we will find new meaning in the individual verses. And when we take up whole portions and meditate upon them, we will find how they lift us up into God's presence and into the life of obedience and joy that says: "I have taken an oath and confirmed it, that I will follow your righteous laws" (v. 106). "Oh, how I love your law! I meditate on it all day long" (v. 97).

Begin to work into your morning prayers the devotional life found in this Psalm. Let God's Word lead you into communion with God every day and before everything else. Make its petitions your own and vow to allow God's Word to make you all the more eager to take that Word to others, whether for awakening souls toward God or strengthening them to follow more diligently in His ways.

—— *The Believer's Daily Renewal*

THE WAY *to the* NEW SONG

❖

I waited patiently for the Lord; and He inclined to me, and heard my cry. . . . He has put a new song in my mouth—praise to our God; many will see it and fear, and will trust in the Lord.

Psalm 40:1, 3 NKJV

*L*isten to the testimony of one who can speak from experience of the sure and blessed outcome of patient waiting on God. True patience is so foreign to our self-sufficient nature, yet so indispensable to our waiting on God. It is an essential element of true faith, and we will once again meditate on what the Word has to teach us concerning it.

The word *patience* is derived from the Latin word for suffering. It suggests the thought of being under the constraint of some power from which we are eager to be free. At first we submit against our will. Then experience teaches us that when it is useless to resist, patient endurance is our wisest alternative. In waiting on God, it is important that we submit not because we are forced to, but because we want to be in the hands of our blessed Father. Patience becomes our highest blessing and our highest grace. It honors God and gives Him time to work His will in us. It is the highest expression of our faith in His goodness and faithfulness. It brings the soul perfect rest in the assurance that God is carrying on His work. It is the evidence of our consent that God deal with us in the way and time that He thinks best. True patience loses self-will to His perfect will.

Patient waiting on God brings a rich reward; the deliverance is sure; God himself will put a new song in your mouth. And if you sometimes feel patience is not your gift, remember it *is* God's gift. Take the prayer from Second Thessalonians 3:5 (NKJV): "Now may the Lord direct your hearts into the love of God and into the patience of Christ."

—— *Waiting on God*

PARTAKERS *of the* DIVINE LIFE

---   ❖   ---

But I have prayed for you . . . that your faith may not fail.

Luke 22:32

All growth in the spiritual life is connected with a clearer insight into what Jesus is to us. The more I realize that Christ must be all to me and that all in Christ is for me, the more I learn to live the true life of faith, which means dying to self to live wholly in Him. The Christian life is no longer the vain struggle to live right, but resting in Christ and finding strength in Him *as* our life, to fight the good fight and gain the victory of faith.

This is especially true of the life of prayer. It too comes under the law of faith alone and is seen in the light of the fullness there is in Jesus. The believer understands that prayer no longer needs to be a matter of anxious care but an experience of what Christ will do for us and in us. Further, prayer is participation on earth in the life of Christ in heaven. We can begin to pray not only trusting in the merits of Jesus and in the intercession by which our unworthy prayers are made acceptable, but also in that close union by which He prays in us and we in Him. He lives in us. Because He prays, we pray. Just as the disciples, when they saw Jesus pray, asked Him to make them partakers of what He knew of prayer, so we, seeing Him as our Intercessor on the throne, know that we participate with Him in the life of prayer.

In the incarnation and resurrection of Jesus, a wonderful reconciliation took place by which man became partaker of the divine nature. But the personal appropriation of this reconciliation in each of His members here below cannot take place without the unceasing exercise of His divine power. In conversion and sanctification, in every victory over sin and the world, there is flowing forth the power of Him who is mighty to save.

—— *Teach Me to Pray*

THE ALL-PREVAILING PRAYER

❖

I tell you the truth, my Father will give you whatever you ask in my name. Until now you have not asked for anything in my name. Ask and you will receive, and your joy will be complete.

John 16:23–24

Until this time the disciples had not asked for anything in the name of Christ, nor had He ever used the expression "ask in my name" among them. The closest they came to the thought was that they met together *in His name.* Here in His parting words, before He is betrayed, Jesus repeats the word *whatever* in connection with His promise concerning answered prayer to teach them, and us, that His name is our only and all-sufficient plea. The power of prayer and the answer depend on the right use of His name.

What is it to take action in the name of another? It is to come with the power of attorney for that person as his representative and substitute. Use of another's name supposes a mutual trust.

When the Lord Jesus returned to heaven, He left His work—the management of His kingdom on earth—in the hands of His followers. He gave them His name by which to draw what they needed to conduct His business. They have the spiritual power to avail themselves of the name of Jesus to the extent to which they yield themselves to live for the interests and work of the Master.

There is no one who abandons himself to live by the name of Jesus who does not receive, in ever-increasing measure, the spiritual capacity to ask and receive in that name whatever he wishes. The bearing of the name of another supposes my having given up my own reputation and with it my own independent life; while at the same time, I have taken possession of all there is in connection with that name.

—— *Believing Prayer*

BLESSED WITH EVERY SPIRITUAL BLESSING

❖

Blessed be the God and Father of our Lord Jesus Christ, who has blessed us with every spiritual blessing in the heavenly places in Christ.

Ephesians 1:3

God has blessed us with every spiritual blessing in Christ. He has set Christ at His own right hand, and made us to sit with Christ as well. The manifold wisdom of God is to be made known through the church to the principalities and powers so that we are equipped for battling the spiritual hosts of wickedness. The life of the Christian, regarded in this spiritual and heavenly aspect, can be lived only in the power of the heavenly world.

As believers, we have been sealed in Christ by the Spirit, and the Spirit opens up our understanding to know what we have been called to by God. By the same Spirit we live a life of abiding access to the Father through Christ. No longer living for ourselves, we join our fellow believers in becoming a dwelling place for God. We are strengthened by the Spirit in the inner man and filled with all the fullness of God.

The believer is to walk in meekness and lowliness of heart, keep the unity of the Spirit, and minister in the power of the Spirit for the building up of the body of Christ in love. He seeks never to grieve the Spirit, but rather to be filled with the Spirit, fulfilling the law of love in his daily life. He is strong in the Lord and in the power of His might to fulfill his part in wrestling with the powers of darkness by use of the Word and prayer.

We all need time, thought, prayer, and quiet waiting on the Spirit of God to catch the vision of our place in Christ and to maintain it. The Spirit-sealed, Spirit-taught, Spirit-strengthened, and Spirit-filled life here described is to be the normal spiritual experience. We must turn away from self and the world and allow God to work out in us His purposes according to the counsel of His will.

—— *The Believer's Call to Commitment*

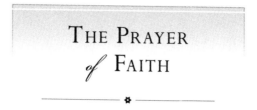

THE PRAYER
of FAITH

❖

And the prayer offered in faith will make the sick person well;
the Lord will raise him up. If he has sinned, he will be forgiven.

James 5:15

*O*nly once does the expression "the prayer offered in faith" occur in the Bible, and it relates to the healing of the sick. The church has adopted this expression, but hardly ever uses it except for obtaining other graces, while according to the Scriptures it is intended for use in praying for the sick.

A question arises: "Does the use of remedies exclude the prayer of faith?" To this I would reply *no*, for the experience of a large number of believers testifies that in answer to their prayers God has often blessed the use of medications and made them a means of healing.

But we also know that under the power of the fall and the realm of our senses, our tendency is to attach more importance to the remedies or medicinal cures than to the direct intervention of God. This is why the Lord in calling Abraham had not recourse to the laws of nature (Romans 4:17–21). God would form for himself a people of faith, living more in the unseen than in things visible; and in order to lead them into this life, it was necessary to take away their confidence in ordinary means.

God wills to act in a similar way with us. The purpose of God is to lead His children into a more intimate communion with Christ, and this is just what happens when by faith we commit ourselves to Him as our sovereign healer, with or without doctors. Healing becomes far more than deliverance from sickness; it becomes a source of spiritual blessing. It makes real to us what faith can accomplish and establishes a new tie between God and the believer; it launches him on a life of confidence and dependence.

—— *Divine Healing*

DO NOT GRIEVE
the SPIRIT

❀

Do not grieve the Holy Spirit of God, by whom you were sealed for the day of redemption.

Ephesians 4:30 NKJV

Isaiah summarized the history of Israel and the Old Testament covenant: "They rebelled and grieved his Holy Spirit" (Isaiah 63:10 NKJV); Stephen, in the New Testament, said: "You always resist the Holy Spirit; as your fathers did, so do you" (Acts 7:51 NKJV). The New Testament standard shows that this should no longer be the case. God promised His people a new heart and a new spirit.

The warning "Do not grieve the Holy Spirit" also contains a promise: What grace commands, it enables us to perform. The believer who desires to live in the consciousness that he has been sealed with the Holy Spirit will find the assurance that the power and presence of the Spirit makes it possible to live without grieving Him.

The work of the Holy Spirit is to reveal Christ to the believer. As a preparation for this revelation, His first job is to convict of the sin of unbelief. The salvation God has prepared for us is comprised in Jesus Christ; the life He lived on earth, of humility and obedience, has been prepared for us and can be received through simple faith alone. The great secret to Christian living lies in the daily unceasing faith in who Jesus is, what He has done for us, and what He provides for us. It roots in us the assurance that He will work in us every moment of our lives. When this faith is not exercised, the Christian life will become ineffective.

Turn to the prayer in the first chapter of Ephesians (vv. 15–23) and see what it teaches us of the need of receiving from the Father the gift of the Spirit of wisdom.

—— *The Believer's Call to Commitment*

THE MOST
WONDERFUL GIFT

* * *

*If you then, being evil, know how to give good gifts to your children,
how much more will your heavenly Father give the Holy Spirit to
those who ask Him!*

Luke 11:13 NKJV

The Father can bestow no higher or more wonderful gift than this: His own Holy Spirit, the Spirit of sonship.

This truth naturally suggests that this first and best gift of God must be the primary object of all prayer. For every need of the spiritual life, the One we must have is the Holy Spirit. All fullness is in Jesus, the fullness of grace and truth out of which we receive grace for grace. The Holy Spirit is the appointed instrument, whose special work it is to make Jesus—and all that is in Him for us—ours in personal appropriation and experience. He is the Spirit of life in Christ Jesus. If we but yield ourselves entirely to the disposal of the Spirit and let Him have His way with us, He will manifest the life of Christ within us. He will do this with divine power, maintaining the life of Christ in us in an uninterrupted flow. Surely if there is one prayer that should draw us to the Father's throne and keep us there, it is for the Holy Spirit, whom we as children have received, to flow in us and from us in greater fullness.

In the variety of the gifts the Spirit dispenses, He meets the believer's every need. He is the Spirit of truth who leads into all truth and makes each word of God ours. He is the Spirit of prayer, through whom we speak to the Father in prayer and are heard.

—— *Teach Me to Pray*

THE SPIRIT *of* SUPPLICATION

❋

In the same way, the Spirit helps us in our weakness. We do not know what we ought to pray, but the Spirit himself intercedes for us with groans that words cannot express. And he who searches our hearts knows the mind of the Spirit, because the Spirit intercedes for the saints in accordance with God's will.

Romans 8:26–27

The Holy Spirit has been given to every child of God. He dwells in him not as a separate being in one part of his nature but as his very life. He is the divine power by which our life is maintained and strengthened. The Holy Spirit can and will work in a believer all that one is called to be or to do. Of course, the person on his part must yield to the Holy Spirit. Without this, the Spirit cannot work and the person's spiritual life will be less than effective. But as he learns to yield, to wait, and to obey the leading of the Spirit, God will work in him all that is pleasing in His sight.

The Holy Spirit, above all, is a Spirit of prayer. He intercedes for the saints in accordance with God's will. As we pray in the Spirit, our worship is as God desires it to be, in spirit and in truth. Prayer is simply the breathing of the Spirit in us; power in prayer comes from the power of the Spirit in us as we wait on Him. Failure in prayer is the result of a human spirit that is not yielded to the Spirit of God. In this sense, prayer is a gauge that measures the work of the Spirit in us. To pray aright, the life of the Spirit must be active in us. For praying the effective, fervent prayer of a righteous man, everything depends on being full of the Spirit.

Each day, accept the Holy Spirit as your guide, your strength, the one who reveals Christ to you, your very life. Unseen but known by faith, He gives all the love, faith, and power for obedience that one needs.

—— *The Ministry of Intercessory Prayer*

THE HIGH-PRIESTLY
PRAYER *of* CHRIST

❁

*"Father, the time has come. Glorify your Son, that your Son may
glorify you. . . . I have brought you glory on earth by completing the
work you gave me to do. . . . I am coming to you now, but I say these
things while I am still in the world, so that they may have the full
measure of my joy within them. . . . My prayer is not that you take
them out of the world but that you protect them from the evil one."*

John 17:1, 4, 13, 15

In His parting address, Jesus gives His disciples a revelation of what their
new life would be when the kingdom of God came to them in power. By the
indwelling of the Holy Spirit, their union with the heavenly Vine, and in
their going forth to witness and to suffer for Him, they would find their true
calling and blessing. While telling them of their new life, He repeatedly gave
unlimited promises as to the power their prayers would have.

To allow His disciples the joy of knowing what His intercession for them in
heaven as their High Priest would be, He gave them the legacy of this prayer to
His Father. At the same time, He wanted them to share in His work of intercession and the prayer would show them how to perform this holy work. From
the Lord alone we can learn what prayer in His name is to be and what it is to
accomplish. To pray in His name is to pray in unity with Him. The high-priestly
prayer teaches what prayer in the name of Jesus can ask and expect to receive.

The prayer is divided into three parts. First, our Lord prays for himself
(vv. 1–5), then for His disciples (vv. 6–19), and finally for all the believing
people through all ages (vv. 20–26). Followers of Jesus dedicated to the work
of intercession will see this prayer as a model.

*Lord, I come to accept this as my calling. For this I would forsake all and follow
you. Into your hands I would yield my whole being in believing trust. Form and train
me to be one of your prayer warriors. Inspire me to be one with the wrestlers who watch
and strive in prayer.*

—— *Teach Me to Pray*

THE HOLY SPIRIT
and PRAYER

❖

But you, dear friends, build yourselves up in your most holy faith and pray in the Holy Spirit. Keep yourselves in God's love as you wait for the mercy of our Lord Jesus Christ to bring you to eternal life.

Jude 20–21

To understand how the coming of the Holy Spirit was to open up a new dimension in prayer, we must remember who He is, what His work is, and the significance of His not being given until Jesus was glorified. It is by the Spirit that the Son was begotten of the Father; it is in the fellowship of the Spirit that the Father and the Son are one. It is especially true now, when the Son as our Mediator ever lives to intercede for us.

This gift of the Father was something entirely different from what the Old Testament saints knew. The redemption of our human nature into fellowship with His power and glory, and the union of our humanity in Christ with the triune God were of such significance that the Holy Spirit, testifying in our hearts what Christ had accomplished, was no longer only as He had been known in the Old Testament.

The continued efficacy and application of our redemption is maintained by the intercession of Christ. It is through the Holy Spirit descending from Christ to us that we are drawn into the great stream of His ever-ascending prayers. The Spirit prays for us without words. In the depths of our hearts, where our thoughts are at times without form, the Spirit takes us into the flow of the life of the triune God. Through the Spirit, Christ's prayers become ours, and ours are made His; we ask what we will, and it is given to us. Now we understand from experience that until now we have not really asked.

My blessed Lord Jesus, help me to understand your teaching that it is the indwelling Spirit, united with you, pouring from you, who is the Spirit of prayer. Teach me to become empty, a wholly consecrated vessel yielded to His leading, honoring and trusting Him as a living person, for that He is.

— *Believing Prayer*

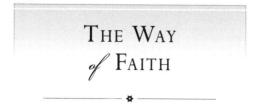

THE WAY
of FAITH

✿

Immediately the boy's father exclaimed, "I do believe;
help me overcome my unbelief!"

Mark 9:24

These words have been a help and strength to thousands of souls in their pursuit of salvation and the gifts of God. Notice that it is in relationship to the fight of faith while seeking healing for an afflicted child that they are proclaimed. We see in them the struggle that can arise between faith and unbelief, and that it is not without some effort that we come to believe in Jesus and in His power to heal.

Take note first that without faith no one can be healed. When the father of the afflicted child said to Jesus, "But if you can do anything, take pity on us and help us," Jesus replied, "Everything is possible for him who believes" (vv. 22–23). Jesus had the power to heal, and He was ready to do it, but He put responsibility on the man.

In order to obtain healing from Jesus, it is not enough to pray. Prayer without faith is powerless. "The prayer offered in faith will make the sick person well" (James 5:15). If you have already asked for healing from the Lord, or if others have asked it for you, you must be able to say with faith, "On the authority of God's Word, I have the assurance that He hears me and that I shall be healed." To have faith for healing means to surrender your body absolutely into the Lord's hands and to leave yourself entirely to Him. Faith receives healing as a spiritual grace that proceeds from the Lord, even while there is no conscious change in the body.

How is such faith to be obtained? Say to Him, "Lord, I am still aware of the unbelief that is in me. Nevertheless, I want to conquer this unbelief. I know, Lord, you will give me the victory. I desire to believe; by your grace, I dare to say I can believe." It is when we are in intimate communion with the Lord, and when our heart responds to His, that unbelief is overcome and conquered.

—— *Divine Healing*

THE SPIRIT *of* LOVE

❋

But the fruit of the Spirit is love, joy, peace, longsuffering, kindness, goodness, faithfulness, gentleness, self-control. Against such there is no law.

Galatians 5:22–23 NKJV

*L*ove is not only the fruit of the Spirit from which all others come, but the Spirit is nothing less than divine Love itself come down to dwell in us, and we have only as much of the Spirit as we have love.

God is a Spirit; God is Love. In these words we have the only attempt Scripture makes to give us, in human language, what may be called a definition of God. (The third expression, God is Light, is a figurative one.)

Everything owes its life to the Spirit of God. This is so because God is Love. It is through the Spirit that the love of God is revealed and communicated to us. It was the Spirit that led Jesus to the work of love for which He was anointed—to preach good news to the poor and deliverance to the captives. Through that same Spirit He offered himself as a sacrifice for us. The Spirit comes laden with all the love of God.

Complaints or confessions of tempers unconquered; selfishness; harsh judgments; unkind words; or a lack of meekness, patience, and gentleness is simply proof that we do not yet understand that to be a Christian is to have the Spirit of Christ, which is the Spirit of Love. Generally, we are more carnal than spiritual.

In faith that the Spirit of Love is within us, let us look to the Father in earnest prayer and plead for His mighty working in our innermost being, that Christ may dwell in our hearts, that we may be rooted and grounded in love, that our whole life might have its nourishment and strength in love.

—— *The Indwelling of the Spirit*

WHO SHALL
DELIVER US?

❁

What a wretched man I am! Who will rescue me
from this body of death? Thanks be to God—
through Jesus Christ our Lord!

Romans 7:24–25

When we speak of a lack of prayer and the desire to live a fuller prayer life, there are many difficulties to be faced. Often we have resolved to pray more and better, and have utterly failed. Our prayers, rather than being full of joy and strength, are often a source of self-condemnation and doubt.

It is important to distinguish between the symptoms of a disease and the disease itself. Weakness and failure in prayer are signs of weakness in the spiritual life. If a patient were to ask a doctor to give him something to stimulate a weak pulse, he would be told that this is not the issue. The pulse is the index of the state of the heart and the whole system. The doctor strives to have health restored, but he must first determine the *cause* of the weak pulse.

God has so created us that the exercise of every healthy function causes joy. Prayer is meant to be as simple and natural to the believer as breathing or working is to a healthy individual. The reluctance we feel and the failure we confess are God's reminders to acknowledge our disease and to come to Him for the healing He has promised.

Your lack of prayer is likely due to a stagnant state of life. Deliverance comes through the Holy Spirit giving the full experience of what the life of Christ can work in us. Do not despair or lose hope; there is a solution. Because there is a Physician, there is healing for our sickness. What is impossible with man is possible with God.

—— *The Ministry of Intercessory Prayer*

WAITING
QUIETLY

❀

It is good that one should hope and wait quietly
for the salvation of the Lord.

Lamentations 3:26 NKJV

As long as waiting on God is thought of only as a step toward more productive prayer and obtaining answers to our requests, we will not know the blessing of time with God for the sake of fellowship with Him. But when we realize that waiting on God is a blessing in itself, our adoration of Him will humble us, making the way open for God to speak to us and reveal himself to us. "The lofty looks of man shall be humbled, the haughtiness of men shall be bowed down, and the Lord alone shall be exalted in that day" (Isaiah 2:11 NKJV).

Everyone who wants to learn the art of waiting on God must be quiet and listen. Take time to be away from friends, from duties, from cares and joys; time to be still before God. Give the Word and prayer high priority; but even these good things may get in the way of simply waiting. The activity of the mind needed to study the Word and to put thoughts into prayer, and the activity of the heart with its desires and hopes and fears, may distract us from waiting on the One who knows our mind and heart. Our whole being is not allowed to become prostrate in silence before Him. Though at first it may be difficult to set aside these activities for a time, every effort to do so will be rewarded. We will find that this kind of waiting gives peace and renewed energy we may not have known.

One reason that it is good to learn to wait quietly before the Lord without speaking is that it acknowledges our inability to receive blessing from God on our own. The blessing will not come by our "willing" or "running," or even by our thinking and praying, but by our waiting in His presence. By waiting we confess our trust that God will in His time and in His way come to our aid.

—— *Waiting on God*

THE DEVOTIONAL LIFE
and COMMITMENT

❋

But you, when you pray, go into your room, and when you have
shut your door, pray to your Father who is in the secret place; and
your Father who sees in secret will reward you openly.

Matthew 6:6 NKJV

We use the word *devotion* in two senses: first, with regard to private prayer, and second, with regard to the spirit of devotion, or commitment to God, which is the mark of our daily life. In our text, we have two thoughts. If in our private prayer we truly meet our Father who sees in secret, He promises us the open reward of grace to live our life to His glory—the whole and continual commitment of our entire personality to His will. The act of commitment in private devotion secures the power for that spirit of commitment that extends through our daily life.

An outstanding passage concerning this principle of commitment or consecration to God is found in Leviticus 27:28: "Nevertheless no devoted offering that a man may devote to the Lord of all that he has, both man and beast, or the field of his possession, shall be sold or redeemed; every devoted offering is most holy to the Lord" (NKJV). The story of Achan (Joshua 6:17–18) is a solemn commentary on how this principle works out: "The city and all that is in it are to be devoted to the Lord. Only Rahab the prostitute and all who are with her in her house shall be spared, because she hid the spies we sent. But keep away from the devoted things, so that you will not bring about your own destruction by taking any of them. Otherwise you will make the camp of Israel liable to destruction and bring trouble on it." *Devoted* here means "committed to God for destruction." The punishment, first on Israel in its defeat and then on Achan, gives a somber illustration of the seriousness in God's sight of devoting or committing something to Him. Commitment is the wholehearted and irrevocable surrendering to God what may never be taken back again. The person or thing consecrated is "most holy to the Lord."

—— *The Believer's Call to Commitment*

THE TRUE
WORSHIPERS

✿

Yet a time is coming and has now come when the true worshipers
will worship the Father in spirit and truth, for they are the kind
of worshipers the Father seeks. God is spirit, and his worshipers
must worship in spirit and in truth.

John 4:23–24

Jesus' words to the woman of Samaria make up His first recorded teaching on prayer. The Father *seeks* worshipers. Our worship satisfies His loving heart and is a joy to Him. He seeks *true worshipers* but does not find many.

Our Lord spoke of three kinds of worship to the woman of Samaria. There is the unlearned worship of the Samaritans: "You Samaritans worship what you do not know" (v. 22); the intelligent worship of the Jew, having the true knowledge of God: "We worship what we do know, for salvation is from the Jews" (v. 22); and the new spiritual worship that He himself came to introduce: "Yet a time is coming and has now come when the true worshipers will worship the Father in spirit and truth" (v. 23). From this connection, it is evident that the words *in spirit and truth* do not mean "from the heart, in sincerity."

The Samaritans had the five books of Moses and some knowledge of God; there was doubtless more than one among them who sincerely sought God in prayer. The Jews had the full revelation of God in His Word as had been given up to that time; there were among them godly men who called upon God with their whole heart. But worshiping "in spirit and truth" had not yet been fully realized.

Among Christians there are still three levels of worshipers: some, in their ignorance, hardly know what they are asking. They pray earnestly but receive little. Others, with more knowledge, try to pray with all their mind and heart, but do not attain the full blessing. We must ask our Lord Jesus to take us to the third level: to be taught of Him how to worship in spirit and truth.

—— *Teach Me to Pray*

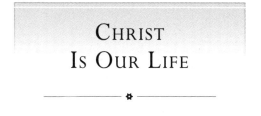

CHRIST
IS OUR LIFE

❁

When Christ, who is your life, appears, then you also will appear with him in glory.

Colossians 3:4

I know that many who have made an absolute surrender have felt as I have: How little I understand it! And they have prayed, "Lord God, if we are to know what it really means, you must take possession of us." By faith God does accept our surrender, although the experience and the power of it may not come at once. We are to hold fast our faith in God until the experience and power do come.

If absolute surrender is to be maintained and lived out, it can only be by having Christ enter our life in new power. *Christ is our life.* We often plead with God to work in the church and in the world that by the power of His Holy Spirit His people might be sanctified and sinners be converted. We must not neglect to pray also for ourselves, so that as Christ takes full possession of us, He will be able to work through us to the end that others might be helped.

Let us yield ourselves to God in prayer that He might search our hearts and reveal to us whether the life of Christ is the law of our life. Many people want eternal life but do not want to live the life here on earth that Christ lived.

Have you felt afraid to make a complete surrender because you felt unworthy? Consider this: Your worthiness is not in yourself or in the intensity of your consecration; *your worthiness is in Christ himself.*

Jesus Christ wants to be your companion so that you will never be alone. There is no trial or difficulty through which you pass without His promise "I will be with you." No battle with sin or temptation, no weakness that makes you tremble at the consciousness of what you are in yourself, excludes the fact that Christ is at your side every moment.

—— *Absolute Surrender*

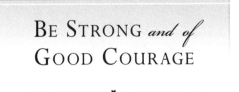

BE STRONG *and of* GOOD COURAGE

❋

Wait on the Lord; be of good courage, and He shall strengthen your heart; wait, I say, on the Lord!

Psalm 27:14 NKJV

The psalmist said in the previous verse, "I would have lost heart, unless I had believed that I would see the goodness of the Lord in the land of the living" (v. 13). If it had not been for his faith in God, he would have given up by his own admission. But in the confident assurance in God that faith gives, he urges himself and us to remember one thing above all: Wait on God. The deliverance we often wait for is from our enemies, in whose presence we feel powerless. The blessings we plead for are spiritual and unseen, things impossible with men. Our heart may well faint and fail. Our souls may hold intimate fellowship with God, but the God we wait on often appears to be hidden.

We are in such a habit of evaluating God and His work in us by what we *feel* that it is very likely that on some occasions we will be discouraged because we do not feel any special blessing. Above everything, when you wait on God, you must do so in the spirit of hope. God in His glory, His power, and His love longs to bless you.

The blessedness of waiting on God has its root in the fact that He is full of goodness, power, life, and joy. God is love! That is the one and only all-sufficient reason for our expectation. Love seeks out its own: God's delight is to impart himself to His children. However weak you *feel,* wait in His presence. As the sun does its work on the weak who seek its rays, God will do His work in you. Trust Him!

—— *Waiting on God*

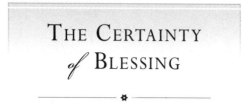

THE CERTAINTY
of BLESSING

❖

*Then you will know that I am the Lord, for they shall not be
ashamed who wait for Me.*

Isaiah 49:23 NKJV

God seeks our fellowship with Him by the most positive assurances. He
says it will *never* be in vain, that those who hope in God will not be disappointed. It is strange that though we should so often have experienced it, we
are still slow to learn that waiting on God must and can be the very breath of
our life, a continuous resting in God's presence and love, a constant yielding
of ourselves to Him to perfect His work in us.

This waiting on God on behalf of His church and His people will depend
greatly on the place that waiting on Him has in our personal life. Our minds
may often have a vision of what God has promised to do, and our tongues
may speak of them in eloquent words, but these are not the measure of our
faith or power. Rather it is what we know of God in our personal experience:
conquering the enemies within, reigning, ruling, and revealing himself in
His holiness and power in our inmost being. It is this revelation that will be
the true measure of the spiritual blessing we expect from Him and that we
will bring to others.

It is as we know how waiting on God can bless our own souls that we will
confidently hope for the blessing to come to the church around us. The promised blessings for us and for others may be delayed, but knowing Him who
has promised makes the wait worthwhile and full of hope. Be sure to allow
this truth to take full possession of your soul: Waiting on God is the highest
privilege of His redeemed child.

—— *Waiting on God*

THE SECRET *of* TRUE OBEDIENCE

— ✿ —

Obey me, and I will be your God and you will be my people. Walk
in all the ways I command you, that it may go well with you.

Jeremiah 7:23

The secret of true obedience, I believe, is a clear and close personal relationship with God. All our attempts to achieve full obedience will fail until we have access to His abiding fellowship. *It is God's holy presence, consciously abiding with us, that keeps us from disobeying Him.*

On earth Christ was a learner in the school of obedience; from heaven He teaches His disciples on earth. The urgent need to receive our orders and instructions continually from God himself is implied in the words "Obey me, and I will be your God." The expression "obey the commandments" is seldom used in Scripture; it is rather "Obey me" or "Obey, listen to *my voice.*"

In learning obedience, Christ used the same textbook as we have. And He appealed to the Word not only when He had to teach or to convince others; He needed it and He used it for His own spiritual life and guidance. To appropriate the Word in His own life and conduct, to know when each particular portion was applicable, Christ needed and received divine teaching. Even so does He teach us by giving us the Holy Spirit as Divine Interpreter of the Word.

The true scholar of a great master finds it easy to render him unwavering obedience because he trusts his teacher so implicitly. The student sacrifices his own wisdom to be guided by a higher wisdom. We need this confidence in our Lord Jesus. Just as we have trusted Him as our Savior to atone for our disobedience, let us trust Him as our teacher to lead us out of it and into a life of practical obedience.

—— *A Life of Obedience*

WITH YOUR
WHOLE HEART

✿

*Trust in the Lord with all your heart, and lean not
on your own understanding.*

Proverbs 3:5 NKJV

The fruit of our waiting depends on the state of our heart. As a man's heart is, so is he before God. We can advance no further or deeper into the Holy Place of God's presence than our heart is prepared for it by the Holy Spirit.

It is with the heart that man believes and comes into contact with God. It is in the heart that God has given His Holy Spirit to reveal the presence and power of God working in us. In our efforts to follow God, it is the heart that must trust, love, worship, and obey Him. The mind is completely incapable of creating or maintaining the spiritual life. It is the heart that must wait on God.

It is the same in the physical life. My mind may dictate what to eat and drink and even understand how the food nourishes me. But reason cannot do the nourishing. The body's organs are for that purpose. And so reason may tell me what God's Word says, but it can do nothing about feeding my soul with the bread of life—the heart alone can do this by faith and trust in God.

Remember the difference between *knowing* with the mind and *believing* with the heart. Beware of the temptation to lean on your natural understanding. Present your heart to Him as that wonderful part of your spiritual nature in which God reveals himself and by which you can know Him. Develop confidence that though you cannot see into your heart, God is working there by His Holy Spirit. Allow the heart to wait at times in perfect silence and quiet; in its hidden depths God will work. Be confident of this. Give your whole heart, with its secret yearnings, into God's hands continually. He wants possession of your heart and He will take it.

—— *Waiting on God*

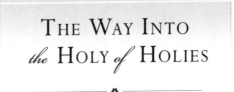

THE WAY INTO
the HOLY *of* HOLIES

❀

*Therefore, brothers, since we have confidence to enter the Most
Holy Place by the blood of Jesus, by a new and living way opened
for us through the curtain, that is, his body, and since we have a
great priest over the house of God, let us draw near to God with a
sincere heart in full assurance of faith.*

Hebrews 10:19–22

The high priest once a year entered into the second tabernacle within the
veil. When Christ died, the veil was rent. All who were serving in the holy
place had free access at once into the most holy. Christ's redemption has opened
the way: Our acceptance of it must lead to nothing less than our entering in.

The priests in Israel might enter the holy place, but were always excluded
from the holiest, God's immediate presence. The rent veil proclaimed liberty
of access into that presence. It is there that believers as a royal priesthood are
now to live and walk. Some say "Let us draw near" refers to prayer, and that in
our special approach to God in acts of worship we enter the holiest. As great
as the privilege of prayer is, God means something infinitely greater for us.
We are to draw near and dwell, that is, live our life and do our work within
the sphere, the atmosphere, of the inner sanctuary. It is God's presence that
makes any place the holiest of all and it is in this presence we are to abide.
There is not a single moment of the day, not a circumstance or atmosphere
that can block the believer's continual dwelling in the secret place of the
Most High. As by faith we enter into the completeness of our reconciliation
with God and the reality of our oneness with Christ, we may draw near with
uninterrupted access.

"The worshipers would have been cleansed once for all, and would no longer
have felt guilty for their sins" (Hebrews 10:2). Walking in the light, the blood
of Jesus cleanses, with a cleansing that never ceases. The liberty to draw near
rests in the never-failing efficacy of the precious blood of Christ.

—— *The Path to Holiness*

WHAT ARE YOU
WAITING FOR?

✿

And now, Lord, what do I wait for? My hope is in You. Deliver me
from all my transgressions.

Psalm 39:7–8 NKJV

There may be times when we do not know what we are waiting for, but we know we need to be in His presence. Other times we *think* we know, and it would be better to simply wait on Him without an agenda. He is able to do for us immeasurably more than all we ask or think, and we are in danger of limiting Him when we confine our desires and prayers to our own thoughts. It is a good thing at times to say with the psalmist, "Lord, what do I wait for?" That is, I hardly know; I can only say, "My hope is in You."

We clearly see a limiting of God in the case of Israel. When Moses promised them meat in the wilderness, they doubted, saying, "Can God prepare a table in the wilderness? . . . He struck the rock, so that the waters gushed out. . . . Can He give bread also? Can He provide meat for His people?" (Psalm 78:19–20 NKJV). If they had been asked whether God could provide streams in the desert, they would have answered *yes.* God had done it; He could do it again. But when there was an idea that God might do something new, they limited Him. Their expectation could not rise beyond past experience. We may also limit God by our concept of what He has promised or what we think He is able to do. Believe that the promises of God we claim have merit beyond our imagination.

In waiting on God, you may grow weary because you don't know what to expect. Ignorance is often a good sign. He is teaching you to leave everything in His hands.

—— *Waiting on God*

CHRIST
OUR MEDIATOR

———— ✿ ————

Make a plate of pure gold and engrave on it . . . Holy to the
Lord. . . . It will be on Aaron's forehead, and he will bear the guilt
involved in the sacred gifts the Israelites consecrate.

Exodus 28:36, 38

We have in this picture a lesson that leads us a step further in the way of holiness. God produces holiness through the One whom He has chosen, whose holiness belongs to us as His brethren, the members of His own body. This holiness has efficacy such that the insufficiency of our best intentions is cleansed. We can have the assurance of being well-pleasing to God.

Earnest seekers after holiness know all that the Word teaches of the atonement and the full pardon it provides. But when they hear that the blessing is received through childlike simplicity, obedience, and surrender, their hearts fail for fear, as though the blessing were beyond their reach. As I pray and worship, and realize how much I lack of that humility and faith that God has a right to demand, I can look up to the High Priest, to the holy crown upon His forehead. The words there help me to believe that the iniquity of my best intentions is borne and taken away. With all my deficiency and unworthiness, I may know that my prayer is acceptable, even a sweet-smelling savor. I may look up to the Holy One and see Him smiling on me for the sake of His anointed Son. The holy crown shall always be on His forehead, that we may be acceptable before the Lord. It is the blessed truth of substitution—One mediator for all, God's way of making us holy. Our worship is holy and acceptable by virtue of the holiness of our Substitute.

—— *The Path to Holiness*

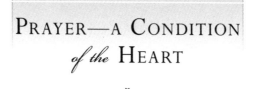

PRAYER—A CONDITION
of the HEART

❖

So you, by the help of your God, return; observe mercy and justice, and wait on your God continually.

Hosea 12:6 NKJV

*I*f waiting on God is the essence of true Christianity, the maintenance of an attitude of entire dependence on Him must be continual. There may be times of waiting for a particular answer, but the attitude and habit of the soul must remain unchangeable and uninterrupted.

Waiting continually *is* a possibility, though many think that our crowded lives make it impossible. They feel they cannot always be thinking of it. This is because they do not understand that it is a matter of the heart and what the heart is full of, what occupies it, even when our thoughts are on other things. A father's heart may be filled continually with intense love and longing for a sick wife or child at home, even though pressing business requires all his thoughts. When the heart has learned how entirely powerless it is to keep itself or to produce any good, when it has learned how surely and absolutely God will keep it, when it has, in despair of itself, accepted God's promise to do for it the impossible, it learns to rest in God and, in the midst of occupations and temptations, waits continually.

Do not limit God by your thoughts of what may be expected. Fix your eyes on this one truth: God in His very nature as the giver of life cannot do otherwise than every moment work in His child. Do not say, "If I wait continually, God will work continually." Rather, turn it around and say, "God works continually; I may wait on Him continually." Take time to catch the vision of God working continually—without a moment's intermission. Then your waiting continually will come naturally. Full of trust and joy, the habit of the soul will be: "On You I wait all the day" (Psalm 25:5 NKJV).

—— *Waiting on God*

HOLINESS
and FAITH

✿

For I have appeared to you for this purpose . . . that they may receive forgiveness of sins and a place among those who are sanctified by faith in me.

Acts 26:16–18

*T*he more we study Scripture in the light of the Holy Spirit or practice the Christian life in His power, the deeper becomes our conviction of the unique and central place faith has in God's plan of salvation. We see, too, that it is fitting and right that it should be so: the very nature of things demands it. Because God is a spiritual and invisible being, every revelation of Him, whether in His works, His Word, or His Son, calls for *faith*. By faith alone we enter into communication with God.

Just as faith is hindered by effort, so is it also by the desire to see and feel. If you believe, you will see. The Holy Spirit will seal our faith with a divine experience; we shall see the glory of God. But this is His work. Ours is when all appears dark, in the face of all that nature or experience testifies, and we still believe in Jesus as our all-sufficiency, in whom we are perfected before God. "The Lord will fight for you" (Exodus 14:14). This thought, so often repeated in connection with Israel's possession of the Promised Land, is the food of faith. In conscious weakness, in the presence of its enemies, it sings the conqueror's song. When God appears not to be doing what we have trusted Him for, then is the time for faith.

Perhaps nothing more fully reveals the true character of faith than joy and praise. Instead of thinking that this life of holiness by faith is a life of difficult attainment and continual self-denial, let us praise God that He has made it possible and certain for us. We can be holy because Jesus is our holiness.

—— *The Path to Holiness*

THE SPIRIT *of* ACCESS

❋

Through him we both have access to the Father by one Spirit.

Ephesians 2:18; cf. 3:12

*H*ere we have the blessed Trinity with the lesson that the great work in which Christ and the Holy Spirit are united is to make the permanent and unceasing presence of God a reality. In the tabernacle, the Holy of Holies was separated by a thick veil from the Holy Place, in which the priest came daily to serve. Not even the High Priest was allowed to enter that Holiest of all, except on one day of the year. Access through the veil was forbidden, punishable by death. When Christ died, the veil was rent in two. Christ Jesus not only entered into God's presence by His blood, but He opened a new and living way through the rent veil of His flesh for every believer to enter. Jesus sent the Holy Spirit from heaven to bring us into that holy presence and to enable us to live in it every day.

As our Advocate, Christ secures our pardon and acceptance. But there is more. Our High Priest lives and acts in the power of an endless, incorruptible life. He works in us by the power of His resurrection life. To have access to God through Christ means that as those "made alive with Christ . . . and seated with him in the heavenly realms" (Ephesians 2:5–7), we live in Him, are one with Him, abide in Him, and are kept by Him in fellowship with God. The access through Christ brings us as near to God as Christ is, in an intimate, divine fellowship that passes all understanding. The Spirit dwells in us to reveal Christ; without Him, no man can truthfully call Jesus Lord. When we yield to Him and trust Him, the Spirit takes control of our life and maintains our fellowship with the Father through the Son.

—— *The Believer's Call to Commitment*

MY EXPECTATION
IS FROM HIM

───────────── ✿ ─────────────

My soul, wait silently for God alone, for my expectation is from
Him. He only is my rock and my salvation; He is my defense;
I shall not be moved.

Psalm 62:5–6 NKJV

There is only one God, one source of life and happiness for the heart. You desire to be good. "No one *is* good but One, that is, God" (Matthew 19:17 NKJV), and there is no possible goodness except what is received directly from Him. You have tried to be holy. "No one is holy like the Lord, for there is none beside You, nor is there any rock like our God" (1 Samuel 2:2 NKJV), and there is no holiness except what He breathes in you by His Spirit. You would live and work for God and His kingdom, for souls and their salvation. "Have you not known? Have you not heard? The everlasting God, the Lord, the Creator of the ends of the earth, neither faints nor is weary. His understanding is unsearchable. He gives power to the weak, and to those who have no might He increases strength. . . . Those who wait on the Lord shall renew their strength" (Isaiah 40:28–29, 31 NKJV).

You will not find many who can help you in this. There will be plenty of fellow Christians who will entice you to put your trust in churches and doctrines, in schemes and plans and human devices, in special men of God, and in special ways of receiving grace. "He removed the high places and broke the sacred pillars, cut down the wooden image and broke in pieces the bronze serpent that Moses had made; for until those days the children of Israel burned incense to it, and called it Nehushtan" (2 Kings 18:4 NKJV). The ark and the temple gave false confidence. Let the living God alone, and none other but Him, be your hope.

No words can tell or hearts conceive the riches of the glory of this mystery of the Father and of Christ. Our God, in the infinite tenderness and almighty power of His love, waits to be our joy and our life.

—— *Waiting on God*

GOD'S CALL *to* HOLINESS

❖

But just as he who called you is holy, so be holy in all you do;
for it is written: "Be holy, because I am holy."

1 Peter 1:15–16

Without doubt, to know what God has called us to is of infinite importance. To misunderstand here could be fatal. You may have heard that God calls you to salvation or to happiness, to receive pardon or to obtain heaven. But have you ever noticed that all these were subordinate to His main purpose? It is to "salvation through sanctification"; to holiness first and foremost as the element in which salvation and heaven are to be found.

No wonder Paul, when he spoke to the Ephesians about being called to be holy, prayed for the spirit of wisdom and revelation in the knowledge of God to be given to each believer that he might know the hope to which he has been called (Ephesians 1:17–18). Our calling, before and above everything else, is to holiness. Let us ask Him to show us what holiness is: first His, and then ours; to show us how He has set His heart upon it as the one thing He wants to see in us: His own image and likeness.

"Just as he who called you is holy, so be holy in all you do" (1 Peter 1:15). This call of God shows us the true motive behind His command "Be holy, because I am holy" (v. 16). It is as if God has said, "Holiness is my glory: without it you cannot see me or enjoy me; there is nothing higher to be had. I invite you to share my likeness." There is nothing better He could offer you.

—— *The Path to Holiness*

THE SPIRIT *of* POWER

❖

For this reason I kneel before the Father, from whom his whole family in heaven and on earth derives its name. I pray that out of his glorious riches he may strengthen you with power through his Spirit in your inner being, so that Christ may dwell in your hearts through faith. And I pray that you, being rooted and established in love, may have power, together with all the saints, to grasp how wide and long and high and deep is the love of Christ.

Ephesians 3:14–18

*O*nce again, we have represented in this wonderful prayer the blessed Trinity: the Father granting the Spirit of power; the Spirit revealing Christ in the heart; that through Christ and the Spirit we may be filled unto all the fullness of God. As God dwells in heaven as the triune One, even so He dwells in our hearts. In speaking of his conversion, Paul says it was the good pleasure of God to reveal his Son in him that he might preach him among the Gentiles. When he preached the unsearchable riches of Christ, he spoke of Him as dwelling in the heart, and he desired that none of his hearers be without that experience. Paul pleaded with God to strengthen them with power in the inner life. Let us begin where Paul begins: In urgent prayer for ourselves and for God's children, let us plead with God that out of His glorious riches he might lift us out of our frail state and bring us into a life that will glorify Him.

It is our responsibility as God's people to receive the strengthening with power according to the riches of His glory. God waits to do it. Who will wait to receive it? What is more, who will yield himself, like Paul, to be an intercessor? Who will plead with and for the believers around him that they may learn to expect the almighty power of God to work in them? Who will plead that what has appeared beyond their reach may become the object of their longing desire and their confident assurance: a life of faith in which Christ truly lives in them.

—— *The Believer's Call to Commitment*

THE FULL BLESSING
of PENTECOST

❋

Do not get drunk on wine, which leads to debauchery. Instead, be filled with the Spirit.

Ephesians 5:18

The command to be filled with the Spirit is just as imperative as the command not to be drunk with wine. And God's command is the sure guarantee that He will give what He desires us to possess. Allow me to suggest some direction for those who desire to receive it.

The full blessing of Pentecost is the inheritance of all the children of God. There are many who do not believe this. They think the day of Pentecost was merely the birthday feast of the church and that it was a time of blessing and power not destined to last. The result is that they never seek to receive the blessing.

In order to carry on her work in the world, the church requires the full blessing of the Spirit. Come to terms with this requirement as a sacred reality. Take time to contemplate this fact and allow yourself to be consumed by the thought of its glorious significance and power. A firm confidence that the blessing is actually within reach is the first step toward obtaining it and a powerful impulse for its pursuit.

There are many believers who think they already have the Holy Spirit and that all they need is to be more faithful in their commitment to know and obey Him. They imagine that they have all that is necessary for continued growth. On the contrary, it is my deep conviction that many are in a state of deception and have need of healing. Just as the first condition of my recovery from a physical illness is to acknowledge that I am sick, so it is absolutely necessary to discover and acknowledge that one does not have the life of Pentecost.

—— *The Fullness of the Spirit*

THE BLOOD
of JESUS

❖

Then He took the cup, and gave thanks, and gave it to them,
saying, "Drink from it, all of you. For this is My blood of the new
covenant, which is shed for many for the remission of sins."

Matthew 26:27–28 NKJV

ear Jesus, unfold to me the secret of your life in me that you gave when you shed
your precious blood on Calvary. Renew afresh this life in me as I partake of the Supper
and drink the cup of remembrance of your great sacrifice. My heart thirsts for you. Come
to me this day in your full power to cleanse anew and fill me with praise for the privilege
that is mine to partake of your life.

Leviticus 17:11 says, "For the life of a creature is in the blood, and I have given it to you to make atonement for yourselves on the altar; it is the blood that makes atonement for one's life." For the blood is the life, the living spirit; and therefore atonement is linked with the shedding of blood. Under the old covenant, it was the life of an innocent animal that was given in the place of a guilty man. And so under the new covenant, the shedding of Jesus' blood meant the surrender of His life for our sins. The worth and power of that blood are the worth and power of the life of Jesus. Every drop of His blood has in it the power of an endless life.

When I partake of that blood, I have a part in the atonement that it established, the forgiveness it secured. I have a part in the life of Jesus, surrendered on the cross, raised from the grave, and now glorified in heaven. The spirit of Jesus' life is the spirit of my life. How powerful, how heavenly must that life be that is nourished by the new wine of the kingdom and communion with the Son. May I ever be thankful that Jesus shed His blood for me.

—— *The Lord's Table*

UNBROKEN FELLOWSHIP

❁

I am crucified with Christ: nevertheless I live; yet not I, but Christ
liveth in me: and the life which I now live in the flesh I live by the
faith of the Son of God, who loved me, and gave himself for me.

Galatians 2:20 KJV

Sometimes we seek for the operation of the Spirit with the purpose of
obtaining more power for work, more love in our life, more holiness in the
heart, more light on Scripture or on our path. But all these gifts are subordinate to the great purpose of God. The Father bestowed the Spirit on the
Son, and the Son gave Him to us for the purpose of revealing and glorifying
Christ Jesus in us.

The heavenly Christ must become for us a real and living personality
who is always with us and in us. Our life on earth can be lived every day
in unbroken fellowship with our Lord Jesus. This is the first and greatest
work of the Holy Spirit in the believer, that we should know and experience Christ as our life.

This was the secret of the joy of the first disciples. They had received the
Lord Jesus—whom they feared they had lost—as the heavenly Christ into
their hearts. And this was their preparation for Pentecost: their attention was
completely taken up with Him. He was literally everything to them. Their
hearts were empty of everything, so that the Spirit could fill them with Christ.
In the fullness of the Spirit they had power for a life and service such as the
Lord desired for them. Is this the goal of our desires and our experience? The
Lord wants us to know that the blessing for which we have so diligently prayed
can be increased in no other way than by the faithful cultivation of intimate
fellowship with Christ in prayer every day.

—— *Living a Prayerful Life*

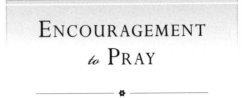

ENCOURAGEMENT
to PRAY

✿

Let us run with perseverance the race marked out for us. Let us fix our eyes on Jesus, the author and perfecter of our faith.

Hebrews 12:1–2

You who are disciples of Jesus and have asked the Master to teach you to pray, accept the lessons He gives. He tells you prayer is the path to faith, a strong faith that can cast out demons. He tells us if we have faith, nothing will be impossible to us. Let this glorious promise be an encouragement to spend more time in prayer.

Teach me, blessed Lord, that there is a place where faith can be learned and gained—in the place of prayer and fasting that brings me into living and abiding fellowship with you and with the Father.

O Savior, you are the author and the perfecter of my faith; teach me what it is to allow you to live in me by your Holy Spirit. Lord, my efforts and prayers for grace to believe have been unavailing. And I know why; I sought for strength in myself. Dear Jesus, teach me the mystery of your life in me, and how you, by your Spirit, undertake to live in me the life of faith, to see to it that my faith shall not fail. Let me see how my faith can be a part of that wonderful prayer life that you give to those who expect their training for the ministry of intercession to come not in word and thought alone, but in the anointing of the Holy Spirit. And teach me how, in fasting and prayer, I may grow into the faith to which nothing is impossible.

—— *Believing Prayer*

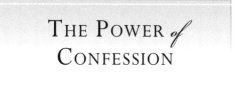

THE POWER *of* CONFESSION

❖

*If we confess our sins, He is faithful and just to forgive us our sins
and to cleanse us from all unrighteousness.*

1 John 1:9 NKJV

It is through faith in the forgiveness of sins that the soul obtains confidence to draw near to the Lord, and thereby also obtain the blessing of a strengthened faith.

Do you believe in the forgiveness of your sins? You know what this means for a Christian. Forgiveness is not the taking away of the sinfulness of the heart, or sanctification, but rather the beginning of the way by which it is to be reached. Forgiveness is the free declaration by which God acquits you of the sins you have committed and no longer counts you guilty. Forgiveness comes first, then sanctification and renewal. For the present, this is the question: Do you believe your sins have been forgiven?

You know what faith is. You know that it is not trusting in your own good works but going to God and finding a resting place in Him and His Word. Consequently, faith that your sins are forgiven is nothing more than the confidence that you, as a sinner, resting in His Word, have come to Him and that your sins have been blotted out. You are indeed blessed if you believe this.

Confess your sins to God, and experience forgiveness now as you spend time in prayer.

—— *The Lord's Table*

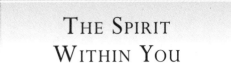

THE SPIRIT
WITHIN YOU

❖

I will give you a new heart and put a new spirit within you. . . .
I will put My Spirit within you and cause you to walk in My
statutes, and you will keep My judgments and do them.

Ezekiel 36:26–27 NKJV

*L*et us join with all who are praying that God may grant a mighty working of the Spirit in His church, that each child of God may prove that in him
the double promise is fulfilled: "I will put a new spirit within you, and I will
put my Spirit within you." Pray that we may apprehend the wonderful blessing of the indwelling Spirit, that our inmost being may be opened to the full
revelation of the Father's love and the grace of Jesus.

God created man's heart for His own dwelling place. Sin entered and de-
filed it. Through the incarnation and atonement of Christ our redemption
was accomplished and the kingdom of God established. Jesus could say, "The
kingdom of God is come unto you; the kingdom of God is *within you*." It is *within*
we must look for the fulfillment of the new covenant; the Spirit of Christ in
us as the power of our life. *Within* us is the true display of the reality and the
glory of His redemption.

O my Father! I thank you that your Spirit dwells in me. Let His indwelling be
in power, in the living fellowship with yourself, in the growing experience of His
renewing power, in the ever fresh anointing that witnesses to His presence and the
indwelling of my glorified Lord Jesus. May my daily walk be in the deep reverence of
His holy presence within me and the glad experience of all He works.

—— *The Indwelling Spirit*

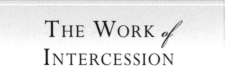

THE WORK *of* INTERCESSION

---❖---

Therefore I exhort first of all that supplications, prayers, interces-
sions, and giving of thanks be made for all men.

1 Timothy 2:1 NKJV

*I*t is only love that can enable us for the work of intercession. That is, the
work of going to God and taking time to lay hold on Him for others. Someone
may be a diligent believer, an eager pastor, a faithful follower, but how often
must one confess that he knows very little of what it is to wait upon God. May
God give us the gift of an intercessory spirit, a spirit of prayer and petition.
Let me challenge you to make it a habit—not to let another day pass without
interceding for God's people.

I know there are believers who think little of true intercession. I find prayer
meetings where they pray for their own members, for their own trials and
troubles, but barely reach beyond their own small group, let alone the world.
Take time to pray for the church citywide, nationwide, and worldwide. It is
only right to pray for the lost. God help us to pray more for them. It is right
to pray for missionaries and for evangelistic work, for the heathen or the unconverted. Paul did say that we must also pray for believers. The condition of
Christ's church is indescribably lacking. Plead for God's people that He would
visit them; plead for each other, and for all believers who seek to do God's
will. Ask Christ to pour His love into you every day. Let love fill your heart.
Receive the Holy Spirit's instruction: *I am set apart to the Holy Spirit, and the*
fruit of the Spirit is love. God help us to grasp this.

—— *Absolute Surrender*

ARE YOU CARNAL
or SPIRITUAL?

❖

*For those who live according to the flesh set their minds on the things
of the flesh, but those who live according to the Spirit, the things of
the Spirit. For to be carnally minded is death, but to be spiritually
minded is life and peace. Because the carnal mind is enmity against
God; for it is not subject to the law of God, nor indeed can be.*

Romans 8:5–7 NKJV

There is a great difference between being carnal (living after the flesh)
and being spiritual. This fact is not always pondered much less understood.
The Christian who walks in the Spirit, and has crucified the flesh, is spiritual
(Galatians 5:24–25). The Christian who walks after the flesh, and wishes to
please the flesh, is carnal (Romans 13:14).

How important it is for us to discover and to clearly acknowledge before
God whether we are spiritual or carnal. A minister may be very faithful in his
teaching of doctrine and be enthusiastic in his service, and yet be such, for the
most part, in the power of human wisdom and zeal. One of the signs of this
is a lack of pleasure or perseverance in fellowship with Christ through prayer.
A love of prayer is one of the marks of the Spirit.

A tremendous change is in store for the carnal Christian who would become
truly spiritual. At first he cannot understand what needs to change or how
it will take place. But the more the truth dawns upon him, the more he is
convinced that it is impossible unless God does the work. Yet to believe that
God will do it requires diligent prayer. Meditation and a quiet, solitary place
are indispensable, along with the end of all confidence in self. But along this
road there comes the faith that God is willing, and He will do it.

How can you say to others, "I, brethren, could not speak to you as to spiritual people but as to carnal, as to babes in Christ" (1 Corinthians 3:1 NKJV)
unless you yourself have the experience of having passed from the one state to
the other? But God will teach you. Persevere in prayer and in faith.

—— *Living a Prayerful Life*

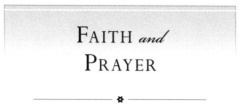

FAITH *and*
PRAYER

❖

In him and through faith in him we may approach God with freedom and confidence.

Ephesians 3:12

Faith is simply surrender: yielding ourselves to the impression of the words we hear. By faith we yield ourselves to the living God. His glory and love fill our hearts and have control over our lives. Faith is fellowship: it is giving ourselves over to the influence of a friend who makes a promise and in that way we become linked to that friend. When we enter into this living fellowship *with God himself,* in the faith that sees and hears Him, it becomes natural to believe His promises regarding prayer. The prayer of faith is rooted in the life of faith.

In this way, the faith that prays effectually is a gift of God. Not as something that He bestows or infuses but as the blessed disposition or habit of soul that is developed in a life of communion with Him. Surely for one who knows his Father well and lives in constant close fellowship with Him, it is a simple thing to believe the promise that He will do what His child asks.

Therefore, surrender to God; allow Him to reveal himself fully in your soul. Count it one of the chief blessings of prayer to exercise faith in God—the living God who waits to fulfill in us all the good pleasure of His will. See Him as the God of love, who delights to bless us and impart himself to us. As we worship God, we will be enabled by His power to believe the promise "Whatever you ask for in prayer, believe that you have received it, and it will be yours" (Mark 11:24). As in faith you make God your own, the promise will be yours as well.

—— *Believing Prayer*

How *the* Spirit
Prepares Us *for* Life

❋

*I pray that you, being rooted and established in love, may have
power, together with all the saints, to grasp how wide and long
and high and deep is the love of Christ, and to know this love that
surpasses knowledge—that you may be filled to the measure of
all the fullness of God.*

Ephesians 3:17–19

I have said before that every blessing God gives is like a seed with the
power of an indissoluble life hidden in it. Let no one think, therefore, that to
be filled with the Spirit is a condition of perfection that leaves nothing more
to be desired. This is in no way the case. It was even after the Lord Jesus was
filled with the Spirit that He had to be further tested and perfected by temptation in order to learn obedience. When the disciples were filled with the
Spirit on the day of Pentecost, power from on high was given them that they
might know victory over sin in their own lives. The Holy Spirit is the Spirit
of truth, and He must guide us into all truth. But it will be step by step that
He leads us. The fullness of the Spirit is preparation for living and working
as a child of God.

From this viewpoint, we see how indispensable it is for every believer to
seek this blessing. Paul offered his prayer in Ephesians on behalf of all believers
without distinction. He did not regard it as a spiritual luxury intended only
for those who were prominent or favored among believers. When he prayed
for them to receive the Spirit, it was for everyone.

Our daily life depends on God's will, His grace, His omnipotence. Every
moment He must work in our inner life and strengthen us by His Spirit in
order that we might live as He would have us live. No creature in the natural
world can exist for a moment without God's sustaining power. Our dependence
must be entirely on God. He alone can finish the work He has begun in us.

—— *The Fullness of the Spirit*

WAITING *for* *the* SPIRIT

❖

On one occasion, while he was eating with them, he gave them this command: "Do not leave Jerusalem, but wait for the gift my Father promised, which you have heard me speak about."

Acts 1:4

*I*n the life of the Old Testament saints, *waiting* was one of the common words by which they expressed the attitude of their souls before God. They waited *for* God and *upon* God. It may be asked whether the text refers to the specific waiting for the outpouring of the Spirit at Pentecost and whether, now that the Spirit has been given to the church, the charge still holds. It could be argued that for the believer who has the Holy Spirit within him, waiting for the promise of the Father is hardly consistent with faith that the Spirit has been received and is already resident.

The question and the argument open the way to a lesson of deepest importance: The Holy Spirit is not given to us as a possession of which we have control. We are not to use Him; He uses us.

Begin in simple faith to cultivate the assurance that *the Holy Spirit is dwelling within you.* Acknowledge the fact with faith and thanksgiving. Each time you enter your place of prayer, be still and remember that the Spirit of prayer that cries "Abba, Father!" is in you.

Now you are in position for taking the second step: Ask God simply and quietly to grant you the mighty *working* of His Holy Spirit (the tending, the molding, the shaping, the influencing) in your life. Rest in what God is going to do, even is doing now, though you may not feel it. Be still before God and give the Holy Spirit time to quicken and deepen in you the assurance of His faithful work.

—— *The Indwelling Spirit*

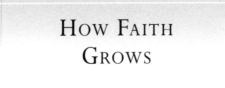

How Faith Grows

❀

You have so little faith. I tell you the truth, if you have faith as small as a mustard seed, you can say to this mountain, "Move from here to there" and it will move. Nothing will be impossible for you.

Matthew 17:20

Faith needs a life of prayer for its full growth. In all the various aspects of the spiritual life, there is such union, such unceasing action and reaction, that each may be both cause and effect. And so it is with faith. There can be no true prayer without faith; some measure of faith must precede prayer. Yet prayer is also the way to more faith; there can be no higher degree of faith except through more prayer.

If we want to know where and how our faith is to grow, the Master points us to the throne of God. It is in prayer, the exercise of faith in fellowship with the living God, that faith can increase. Faith can live only as it is nurtured by God himself.

It is as we take His Word, bringing it before Him, asking Him to make it living and real to us, that the power will come to fully believe it and receive it as our own. It is in prayer, in living contact with the living God, that faith to trust God and to accept all that He says will become real to us.

If we would commit ourselves to the work God has for us in the world, we would soon comprehend the need for much faith and much prayer—the soil in which faith can be cultivated. Christ Jesus is not only our life, He is the life of our faith. It is His life in us that makes us strong enough and simple enough to believe.

—— *Believing Prayer*

A LIFE THAT COUNTS *for* GOD

❋

Now unto him that is able to do exceeding abundantly above all that we ask or think, according to the power that worketh in us, unto him be glory in the church by Christ Jesus throughout all ages, world without end.

Ephesians 3:20–21 KJV

The person who would work with power for others must know the power of God in his own soul. Let every believer's heart cry out with the earnest prayer: *Lord, may your Spirit rest upon me and never depart. Prove your mighty power in my life day by day, in such a way that others will see that God is almighty to save and to keep.*

We desire that our lives would count for God. Are we laboring with a joyful countenance, with a heart full of hope and buoyant expectancy? Cry to God for a great revival in your midst. It is the unceasing prayer of my heart that God would revive His believing people. When I think of all the unconverted in our churches, the skeptics, the wayward, and the perishing around us, my heart cries, "My God, revive your church; revive your people!" However weak some believers may be, if they are children of God, they are your brothers and sisters. We must, then, pray for them, helping them out of darkness and out of the prison in which they find themselves. Our omnipotent God will do in us more than we can ask or think. Paul ascribed glory to Him who is able to do exceeding abundantly above all that we can imagine.

Come together with new consecration, new hope, new courage, and new joy. Believe that God Almighty is with you and at work in you.

—— *Absolute Surrender*

BE FILLED WITH
the SPIRIT

———————— ✿ ————————

If ye love me, keep my commandments. And I will pray the Father,
and he shall give you another Comforter, that he may abide with
you for ever.

John 14:15–16 KJV

Are you willing to pray "O Lord, let me be filled with the Holy Spirit; I surrender anything and everything to you"?

Each of us must examine our own heart. Some have never thought it a necessity to do so. Some have never understood what it meant when Jesus said, "If anyone comes to Me and does not hate his father and mother, wife and children, brothers and sisters, yes, even his own life also, he cannot be My disciple" (Luke 14:26 NKJV). Simply put, our love for God must be greater than the love all of these relationships represent. Surely our lack of victory over sin and the reason the Holy Spirit does not fill us is because we have not forsaken all to follow Christ.

The apostles were men who had accepted the promise of the Spirit from Jesus by faith. On the night before the crucifixion, Christ had spoken to them about the Holy Spirit more than once, and when He was ready to ascend into heaven, He said again, "In a few days you will be baptized with the Holy Spirit" (Acts 1:5). If you had asked those disciples, "What does that mean?" I am sure they could not have told you. But they took the word of Jesus, and if they had any occasion to discuss the subject, I am sure they said something like "If while He was on earth He did such marvelous things for us, now that He is in glory will He not do things infinitely more wonderful?" And they waited for that.

You also must accept this promise by faith and say, "The promise of the filling of the Holy Spirit is for *me*. I accept it from your hand, Lord Jesus." Are you ready by faith to trust the promise, and the Word, and Jesus' love for you?

—— *Absolute Surrender*

DAILY
EXERCISE

❋

He shall be like a tree
Planted by the rivers of water,
That brings forth its fruit in its season,
Whose leaf also shall not wither;
And whatever he does shall prosper.

Psalm 1:3 NKJV

Daily renewal suggests an exercise of utmost importance: solitude and quiet, a true spirit of prayer, devotional reading of God's Word, and fellowship with God (for which the preceding are intended and by which alone they bring blessing). These (preferably morning) exercises are meant to strengthen and equip us for daily interaction with the world as well as service for the kingdom of God in soul-winning and intercession. The motives alone make our devotional time a source of joy and strength.

In my country, there are various diseases that affect our orange trees. One of them is popularly known as "the root disease." While a tree is still bearing fruit, an ordinary observer may not notice anything wrong, but an expert can detect the beginnings of a slow death.

The spiritual life of many Christians suffers from a root disease as well. It is the neglect of secret communion with God. The lack of private prayer, the neglect of the maintenance of the hidden life in Christ, which is rooted and grounded in love, explains the inability of Christians to resist the temptations of this world and to bring forth abundant fruit. Nothing can change this but the restoration of the place of prayer in the life of the believer. As Christians learn not to trust their own efforts but to daily abide deeper into Christ and to make secret personal fellowship with God their goal, true godliness will flourish. "If the root is holy, so are the branches" (Romans 11:16 NKJV). If the morning hour is holy to the Lord, the day with its responsibilities will be so as well.

—— *The Believer's Daily Renewal*

AT THIS MOMENT

❀

Behold, now is the accepted time; behold, now is the day of salvation.

2 Corinthians 6:2 NKJV

Each time your attention is free to occupy itself with thoughts of Jesus—whether it is with time to think and pray or only for a few passing seconds—let your heart say, "Now, at this moment, I do abide in Jesus." Do not use the time in vain regrets that you have not been abiding fully, or in still more hurtful fears that you will not be able to abide, but rather take the position the Father has given you: "I am in Christ; this is the place God has given me. I accept it; here I rest; abiding in Jesus." This is the way to learn to abide continually.

Attainment to the life of perfect abiding is not ordinarily given at once; it comes step by step. Avail yourself, therefore, of every opportunity to exercise the trust available at the present moment.

Each time you bow in prayer, let there be the conscious thought *Father, I am in Christ; I now abide in Him.* In the midst of busyness, when you have the opportunity of self-recollection, may your first involuntary declaration be *I am still in Christ; I abide in Him now.* Even when overtaken by sin, and your heart is disturbed and distracted, let your first look and confession be upward: "Father, I have sinned, and yet I come to you as one who is in Christ. Here I am! I can take no other place; I am in Christ. I *now* abide in Christ." Yes, Christian, in every possible circumstance, every moment of the day, His voice is calling, "Abide in me; abide in me now."

—— *Abiding in Christ*

PERFECT RECONCILIATION

❖

For all have sinned, and come short of the glory of God; Being justified freely by his grace through the redemption that is in Christ Jesus: Whom God hath set forth to be a propitiation through faith in his blood, to declare his righteousness for the remission of sins that are past, through the forbearance of God; To declare, I say, at this time his righteousness: that he might be just, and the justifier of him which believeth in Jesus.

Romans 3:23–26 KJV

So perfect is the reconciliation and so completely has sin been covered and blotted out that he who believes in Christ is looked upon and treated by God as entirely righteous. The acquittal that he has received from God is so complete that there is nothing, absolutely nothing, to prevent him from approaching God with the utmost freedom.

For the enjoyment of this blessedness nothing is necessary except faith in the blood of Christ. The precious blood has been shed, reconciliation is complete, and the message comes to you: "Be reconciled to God."

If you repent of your sins and desire to be delivered from the power and bondage of sin, exercise your faith in the blood of Jesus Christ. Open your heart to the influence of the word that God has sent to you. Open your heart to the message that the blood of Christ can deliver you; yes, even you, this very moment. Only believe it. Declare, "That precious blood is also for me." If you come as a guilty, lost sinner, longing for pardon, you may rest assured that the blood that has already made a perfect reconciliation covers your sin and restores you immediately to the favor and love of God.

Right now, bow before God and tell Him that you do believe in the power of Christ's blood for your own soul. Having said that, stand on it, hold to it. Through faith in His shed blood, Jesus Christ will reconcile you to God.

—— *The Blood of Christ*

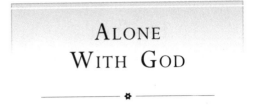

ALONE
WITH GOD

❖

Pray to your Father who is in the secret place; and your Father who sees in secret will reward you openly.

Matthew 6:6 NKJV

The power to maintain close fellowship with God all day will depend entirely upon the intensity with which we seek to secure it in the hour of secret prayer. The one essential in the morning watch is fellowship with God.

Our Lord teaches that this is the secret of private prayer: Close the door and pray to your Father, who is unseen. The first objective is to see that you have the Father's attention and presence. Know that He sees and hears you. Of more importance than all your effort to pray in the right way is this: that you have the childlike assurance that your Father sees you and that as you look on Him, He looks on you, and you enjoy genuine communion with God.

What a difference it would make if everything in our prayer life were subject to this one goal: *I want through the day to walk with God.* What strength would be imparted by the awareness that God has taken charge and He is going with me; I am going to do His will all day in His strength; I am ready for all that might come. What purpose would fill our life if secret prayer were not only asking for comfort or light or strength but also the surrendering of our life for the day into the safekeeping of our Almighty and faithful God.

When secret fellowship with the Father in spirit and in truth is maintained, our public life before others will manifest the reward. The Father who sees in secret takes charge and rewards us openly. Separation from others for a time, in solitude with God, is the only sure way to associate with others in the power of God's blessing.

—— *A Life of Obedience*

WILL YOU BE
MADE WHOLE?

❖

*When Jesus saw him lying there, and knew that he already had been
in that condition a long time, He said to him, "Do you want to be
made well?" The sick man answered Him, "Sir, I have no man to
put me into the pool when the water is stirred up; but while I am
coming, another steps down before me." Jesus said to him, "Rise,
take up your bed and walk." And immediately the man was made
well, took up his bed, and walked.*

John 5:6—9 NKJV

In the Christian life, just as in the physical life, powerlessness to walk is a
symptom of some severe lack in the spirit (or the body) that needs a physician's
attention. This lack of power to walk joyfully in the new and living way that
leads to the Father and the throne of grace is especially devastating. Christ is
the great Physician, who comes to every Bethesda where the sick are gathered
and speaks out His loving, searching question: "Do you want to get well?"

For all who are still clinging to their hope in the pool, or are looking for
someone to place them there, for those who are hoping to be helped somehow
by the continued use of ordinary means of grace, His question points to a better
way. He offers them healing by a way they have never understood. To all who are
willing to confess not only their own powerlessness but also their failure to find
anyone to help them, His question brings the sure and certain hope of deliverance.

But beware of forming wrong expectations of what must take place. When the
man at the pool was made whole, he still had to learn everything about how to
use his new strength. Do not expect to be all at once proficient in prayer or any
part of the Christian life. Only be confident that as you have trusted yourself to
Christ to be your spiritual health and strength, He will guide you and teach you.

Begin to pray. You must start. Count on the fact that He will work in you
what you need. Rise and walk each day in the confidence that He is with you
and will help you.

—— *The Ministry of Intercessory Prayer*

"FOLLOW ME"

❖

And Jesus said to Simon, "Do not be afraid. From now on you will catch men." So when they had brought their boats to land, they forsook all and followed Him.

Luke 5:10–11 NKJV

*T*he holy art of winning souls, of loving them and leading them to the Savior, can be learned only in a close and consistent relationship with Christ. What a lesson for pastors, Christian laymen, and others. This intimate relationship was the great and particular privilege of Jesus' disciples. The Lord chose them that they might learn from Him and carry on His work.

How amazing it is that the Lord Jesus himself wants to train us to be like Him so that others may learn from us. Then we will be able to say with Paul, "Imitate me, just as I also imitate Christ" (1 Corinthians 11:1 NKJV).

Never has a teacher taken such pains with his scholars as Jesus Christ will with those who would preach His Word. He will spare no trouble; no time will be too limited or too long for Him. In the love that took Him to the cross, He wants to fellowship and converse with us, fashion us, sanctify us, and make us fit for His holy service. Dare we still complain that it is too much for us to spend an hour in prayer? Will we not commit ourselves entirely to the love that gave up all for us and look upon daily fellowship with Him as our greatest joy? He calls all you who long for blessing in your ministry to abide in Him. Let it be the greatest delight of your life to spend time with the Master; it will be the surest preparation for fruitful service.

—— *Living a Prayerful Life*

THE INNER LIFE

❖

A little while longer and the world will see Me no more, but you will see Me. Because I live, you will live also. At that day you will know that I am in My Father, and you in Me, and I in you.

John 14:19–20 NKJV

The great characteristic of the New Testament is that it is a dispensation of the inner life. The promise of the new covenant is "I will put My law in their minds, and write it on their hearts" (Jeremiah 31:33 NKJV); "I will give you a new heart and put a new spirit within you" (Ezekiel 36:26 NKJV). The promise of our Lord Jesus was "The Spirit of truth . . . dwells with you and will be in you. . . . At that day you will know that I am in My Father, and you in Me, and I in you" (John 14:17, 20 NKJV). It is in a heart into which God has placed the Spirit of His Son, a heart in which the love of God is shed abroad, that true salvation is found. The place of private prayer with its secret communion with the Father "who sees in secret" is the symbol and the training school of the inner life. Sincere and faithful daily use of the place of prayer will make the inner hidden life strong and full of joy.

In all our efforts at practicing Christianity, the temptation is to give more time and interest to outward means than to inward reality. It is neither the intensity of your Bible study nor the frequency or fervency of your prayers or good works that necessarily constitute a true spiritual life. God is a Spirit, and our spirit within can commune with Him. The way to become conformed to His likeness and partake of His disposition is to spend time in His presence and appropriate His life for your life.

—— *The Believer's Daily Renewal*

DWELLING *in the* HOLY PLACE

❋

Therefore, brethren, having boldness to enter the Holiest by the
blood of Jesus, by a new and living way which He consecrated
for us, through the veil, that is, His flesh, and having a High
Priest over the house of God, let us draw near with a true heart in
full assurance of faith, having our hearts sprinkled from an evil
conscience and our bodies washed with pure water.

Hebrews 10:19–22 NKJV

Let us draw near to God with a true heart in full assurance of faith. The invitation comes to all believers. Do not be satisfied to merely stand on the porch. It is not sufficient to cherish the hope that your sins are forgiven. Let us enter within the veil, let us in spirit press on to greater nearness to our God. Let us make our abode in His holy presence.

It is not as though we as priests were not always in the Holy Place, but there are moments of more immediate fellowship, when the soul turns itself entirely to God to be engaged with Him alone. Too often our prayer consists of calling out to God from a distance; there is little power in it. Before prayer, be sure you are truly in the Holy Place. Be sure your heart is sprinkled from a guilty conscience, and in full assurance of faith appropriate the blood of Christ, by which sin that separates between God and you is entirely removed. Then you can lay your desires and wishes before your Father in full assurance that they are acceptable incense. He who dwells in the Holy Place through the power of the blood is truly one of God's saints, and the power of God's presence is felt around him.

Let us draw near to God; let us pray for ourselves and for one another. Let the Holy Place become our permanent dwelling so that everywhere we go we carry about with us the presence of God. Let this be the fountain of life for us, which grows from strength to strength and from glory to glory.

—— *The Blood of Christ*

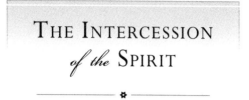

THE INTERCESSION
of the SPIRIT

❖

Likewise the Spirit also helps in our weaknesses. For we do not know what we should pray for as we ought, but the Spirit Himself makes intercession for us with groanings which cannot be uttered.

Romans 8:26 NKJV

What a privilege to be the temple out of which the Holy Spirit cries to the Father and offers His unutterable intercession, too deep for words. Believe in the certainty of the Holy Spirit's working and praying in you in a way that no human mind can apprehend. Believe that in the secret, quiet steadiness of that work, His almighty power is perfecting the divine purpose and the divine oneness with your blessed Lord. Live as one in whom the things that pass all understanding have become truth and life, and through the intercession of the Spirit have become part of your daily life in Christ.

O my Father, you know that I can scarcely take in the wondrous thought that your Holy Spirit actually dwells in me and prays through my frail prayers. May both my inmost being and my outward life be under the Spirit's leading to the extent that I may have the spiritual understanding that knows how to ask according to Thy will, and the living faith that receives what it asks. When I know not what or how to pray, O Father, teach me to bow in silent worship and keep waiting before you, knowing that the Spirit breathes the wordless prayer that you alone can understand.

Blessed God, I am a temple of the Holy Spirit. I yield myself that He might use me in the spirit of intercession. May my whole heart be filled with the longing for Christ's honor and His love for the lost that my life might become one unutterable cry for the coming of your kingdom. Amen.

—— *The Indwelling Spirit*

OUR EVERYDAY SALVATION

❖

For this reason I kneel before the Father, from whom his whole family in heaven and on earth derives its name. I pray that out of his glorious riches he may strengthen you with power through his Spirit in your inner being.

Ephesians 3:14–16

Every believer has the right to say each morning, "My Father will strengthen me today with His power as He is strengthening me even now in my inmost being through His Spirit." Each day we are to be content with nothing less than the indwelling of Christ by faith, a life rooted in love and strengthened to know more of the love of Christ. Each day God is filling us afresh with all the fullness of God as we walk in obedience. We can be strong in God's power, giving Him glory in Christ, for He is "able to do immeasurably more than we ask or imagine, according to His power that is at work within us" (v. 20).

We bow to God the Father in the name of the Son. We ask Him to strengthen us through the Spirit for one purpose: that Christ may dwell in our hearts. The whole heart becomes the scene of the blessed operation of the Trinity through the inner and outer life. As our hearts grasp this truth, we give glory, through Christ, to Him who does more than we can ask or imagine by His Holy Spirit.

What a wonderful salvation is wrought in our hearts: the Father breathing His Spirit into us, daily fitting us to be the home of Christ; the Holy Spirit ever revealing and forming Christ within us so that His very nature, disposition, and character become ours; and the Son imparting His life of love and leading us on to be filled with all the fullness of God.

This is our everyday salvation—the Trinity working in us the power and faith of God! Let us worship and wait on Him; let us believe Him and give Him glory.

—— *The Believer's Daily Renewal*

REINFORCING WHAT
the LORD HAS SPOKEN

❁

*Then Manoah prayed to the Lord, and said, "O my Lord, please
let the Man of God whom You sent come to us again and teach us
what we shall do for the child who will be born."*

Judges 13:8 NKJV

An angel of the Lord had appeared to Manoah's wife to predict the birth
of a child. He would be a Nazarite unto God from his birth and a deliverer of
God's people. The first impression Manoah had upon receiving the news from
his wife was that to train such a God-given child for God's service, God-given
grace would be needed.

Manoah's sense of need found its first expression in prayer. Instead of allowing his sense of unworthiness and unpreparedness to depress him, or the
weight of his obligation to push him to do it in his own strength, he simply
prayed. Apparently, to him, prayer was the solution when faced with a difficulty; it was a source of wisdom and strength.

There is an interesting detail about Manoah's prayer: After his wife told him
of the injunctions given by the angel, he still asked for guidance. He wanted
to hear the words for himself, to have full certainty and perfect clarity. The
answer to Manoah's prayer contained no new revelation; it simply pointed
back to the instruction already given: "Of all that I said to the woman let her
be careful. . . . All that I commanded her let her observe" (vv. 13–14 NKJV).
The answer to our own prayer may contain no new truth; no new thought
may be impressed upon our minds. But the reinforcement of what the Lord
has already spoken and the principles laid down in Scripture brought afresh
to our minds is a rich blessing.

—— *Raising Your Child to Love God*

An Example *of* Confident Prayer

Now this is the confidence that we have in Him, that if we ask anything according to His will, He hears us.

1 John 5:14 NKJV

Just as God gave the apostle Paul as an example in his prayer life for Christians of all time, so in our times He gave George Mueller as proof to His church how literally and wonderfully He still hears and answers prayer. Not only did God give this man of God over a million pounds sterling in his lifetime to support his orphanages, but Mueller also stated that he believed the Lord had given him more than thirty thousand souls in answer to prayer. When asked on what ground he so firmly believed this, his answer was, "There are five conditions that I always endeavor to fulfill. In observing these, I have the assurance of an answer to my prayer:

1. I have not the least doubt, because I am assured that it is the Lord's will to save [the souls for which I pray], for He wills that all men should be saved, and come to the knowledge of the truth. Also, we have the assurance 'that if we ask anything according to His will, He hears us.'
2. I have never pleaded for their salvation in my own name, but in the blessed name of my precious Lord Jesus, and on His merits alone.
3. I always firmly believed in the willingness of God to hear my prayers.
4. I am not conscious of having yielded to any sin, for if I regard iniquity in my heart, the Lord will not hear me when I call.
5. I have persevered in believing prayer for more than fifty-two years for some, and shall continue till the answer comes: 'Shall not God avenge his own elect who cry out day and night to Him?'(Luke 18:7 NKJV)."

The way George Mueller walked is the living way to the throne of grace, which is open to all of us.

—— *Living a Prayerful Life*

A Prayer *for* Humility

❖

Thus says the High and Lofty One who inhabits eternity, whose name is Holy: "I dwell in the high and holy place, with him who has a contrite and humble spirit."

Isaiah 57:15 NKJV

The secret of secrets is this: Humility is the soul of true prayer. Until the spirit of the heart is renewed, until it is emptied of all earthly desires and stands in a habitual hunger and thirst after God, which is the true spirit of prayer; until then, all our prayer will be more or less like giving lessons to students: we will mostly say them only because we dare not neglect them.

Stand unchangeably, at least in your desire, in this form or state of heart; it will sanctify every petition that comes out of your mouth; and when anything is read or sung or prayed that is more exalted than your heart is, if you make this an occasion of further identifying with the spirit of the tax collector, you will then be helped and highly blessed by those prayers and praises that seem to belong to a heart better than yours. The tax collector cast down his eyes and could only say, "God be merciful to me, a sinner."

This, my friend, is the secret of secrets. It will help you to reap where you have not sown and will be a continual source of grace in your soul; for everything that inwardly stirs you or outwardly happens to you becomes good to you if it finds you in this humble state of mind. For nothing is in vain or without profit to the humble soul; it stands always in a state of divine growth, and everything that falls upon it is like dew from heaven. And then, whether you are in the church or out of the church, hearing the praises of God or receiving wrongs from men and the world, all will be as edification, and everything will help promote your growth in the life of God.

—— *Humility*

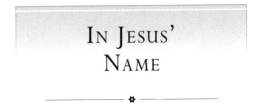

In Jesus'
Name

❊

Whatever you do in word or deed, do all in the name of the Lord
Jesus, giving thanks to God the Father through Him.

Colossians 3:17 NKJV

One of the first conditions of acceptable prayer is fulfilled in it when, as the fruit of its union with Christ, the whole mind is brought into harmony with that of the Son as He said, "Father, glorify Your name" (John 12:28 NKJV).

Abiding in Christ, we can freely use the name of Christ. Asking in the name of another means that person has authorized me and sent me to ask. The person doing the asking wants the favor done for him. Believers often try to think of the name of Jesus and His merits, and to talk themselves into the faith that they will be heard, while they painfully acknowledge how little faith they have in His name. They are not living wholly in Jesus' name. This is obvious because it is only when they begin to pray that they want to take up His name and use it. But this is not what Scripture teaches. The promise "Whatever you ask in My name" (John 14:13 NKJV) cannot be separated from the command "Whatever you do in word or deed, do all in the name of the Lord Jesus."

To Christ, the Father refuses nothing. Abiding in Christ, I come to the Father as one with Him. His righteousness, as well as His Spirit, is in me; the Father sees the Son in me, and gives me my petition. It is not—as so many think—that the Father looks upon us *as if we were in Christ,* even when we are in fact, not in Him. No, the Father wants to see us *living in Him.* In this way our prayer will actually have the power to prevail.

—— *Abiding in Christ*

158

A PERFECT
PRIESTHOOD

❀

But you are a chosen generation, a royal priesthood, a holy nation,
His own special people, that you may proclaim the praises of Him
who called you out of darkness into His marvelous light.

1 Peter 2:9 NKJV

The blood of Jesus carries with it His victory over sin and death. It, in turn, inspires us with a consciousness of His power to conquer sin and every enemy. Jesus, the living, priestly King upon the throne, cannot manifest His full power in us by exercising it from above or from the outside, but only by His indwelling presence. As King and High Priest, He takes up His abode within us and makes us kings and priests.

Do you want to know the purpose of this? The answer is not hard to find. Why is Jesus seated as a priest on the throne of heaven? So that man may be blessed and that God may be glorified in him. As High Priest, He lives only for others, to bring them near to God. He lives as King only that He might reveal the kingdom of God in us and through us. He makes us priests that we might serve the living God as well, that we might be filled with His Spirit so as to be a blessing to others.

As priests through the blood of Christ we live to pray for others, to work among them, to teach them, and to bring them to God. To be a priest is not an idle, self-seeking occupation. It is a compelling power to enter into God's presence on behalf of those in and out of the kingdom. It is the power to pray for blessings, to receive them and to distribute them. The Christian who yields himself to be made a king by Christ lives in the joyous certainty that he is one with Him who has won the victory, and that in Him he is more than conqueror.

—— *The Blood of Christ*

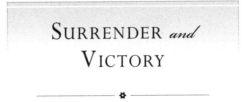

SURRENDER *and* VICTORY

❋

Thanks be to God who always leads us in triumph in Christ, and through us diffuses the fragrance of His knowledge in every place.

2 Corinthians 2:14 NKJV

*O*ur prayer life is not something that can be improved upon in and of itself. So intimately is it a part of the entire spiritual life that only when that whole life (previously marked by a lack of prayer) becomes renewed and sanctified can prayer have its rightful place of power. We must not be satisfied with less than the victorious life to which God calls His children.

How do we attain victory? It all depends on our right relationship to Christ, our complete surrender, unwavering faith, and unbroken fellowship with Him.

You may have used the words *surrender* and *consecration* many times but without a right understanding of their full meaning. If you have been brought by the teaching of Romans 7 ("For what I am doing, I do not understand. . . . what I will to do, that I do not practice . . . what I hate, that I do") to a sense of the hopelessness of leading a Christian life or a prayer life by your own efforts, you will begin to realize that the Lord Jesus must take possession of you by His Spirit to an entirely new degree. This alone can preserve you from continual sin. You will begin to look away from yourself, be free from yourself, and to expect everything to come from the Lord Jesus. Only then will you be truly victorious.

When we begin to understand this, we will admit that in our nature there is nothing good; we have been nailed with Christ to His cross. We will come to see what Paul means when he says that we are dead to sin by the death of Christ. We also share in the glorious resurrection life that is in Him.

—— *Living a Prayerful Life*

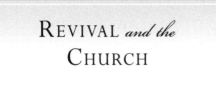

REVIVAL *and the* CHURCH

❖

Come, and let us return unto the Lord: for he hath torn, and he will heal us; he hath smitten, and he will bind us up. After two days will he revive us: in the third day he will raise us up, and we shall live in his sight.

Hosea 6:1–2 KJV

*A*ll those who pray for and claim in faith God's reviving power for His church must humble themselves in full confession of sins. Need of revival always points to previous decline, and decline is always caused by sin. Humiliation and contrition have always been the conditions for revival. In all intercession, confession of man's sin and declaration of God's righteous judgment are essential elements.

The letters to the seven churches (in the book of Revelation) show us five churches of which God, out of whose mouth goes the sharp two-edged sword, says He has something against. In each of these, the keyword of His message is not to the unconverted but to the church: "Repent!" All the glorious promises each of these letters contain share one condition, right down to the invitation, "Open the door and I will come in," and the promise, "He that overcomes will sit with me on my throne." All are dependent on the one word: "Repent!"

Is there not in the church of our day an idolatry of money and talent and culture—unfaithfulness to its one husband and Lord, and a confidence in the flesh that grieves and resists God's Holy Spirit? And is there not a common confession of a lack of spirituality and spiritual power?

Until those who would lead the church in the path of revival bear faithful testimony against the sins of the church, it is likely that it will find people unprepared. Most would prefer to have a revival as the result of their programs and efforts. God's way is the opposite. Out of death, acknowledged as the wage of sin, and confession of utter helplessness, God revives.

—— *The Ministry of Intercessory Prayer*

INTERCESSORY PRAYER *of* FAITH

How much more shall the blood of Christ, who through the eternal Spirit offered himself without spot to God, purge your conscience from dead works to serve the living God?

Hebrews 9:14 KJV

The ministry of intercession is one of the highest privileges of the child of God. To be clear, it does not simply mean that we have determined there is a need in the world or in some particular person and so we pour out our prayer to God for it or them. That is good, so far as it goes, and brings a blessing with it. But the peculiar ministry of intercession is something more than that and finds its power in "the prayer of faith." This prayer of faith is different from pouring out our wishes to God and leaving them with Him.

In the true prayer of faith, the intercessor must spend time with God to appropriate the promises of His Word, and must permit himself to be taught by the Holy Spirit as to whether the promises can be applied to this particular case. He takes upon himself as a burden the sin and need that are the subjects of his prayer, and lays hold of the promise concerning it as though it were for himself. He remains in the presence of God until the Spirit awakens faith in his heart that in this matter the prayer has been heard.

In this way parents sometimes pray for their children, others for the ministers of their church, for laborers in God's vineyard and the souls committed to them, until they know that their prayer is heard. It is the blood of Christ through its power in bringing us near to God that bestows such liberty to pray until the answer is obtained.

— *The Blood of Christ*

THE HOLY SPIRIT
and the CROSS

❖

Christ has redeemed us from the curse of the law, having become a curse for us (for it is written, "Cursed is everyone who hangs on a tree"), that the blessing of Abraham might come upon the Gentiles in Christ Jesus, that we might receive the promise of the Spirit through faith.

Galatians 3:13–14 NKJV

The Holy Spirit always leads us to the cross. It was so with Christ. The Spirit taught Him and enabled Him to offer himself without spot or blemish to God.

It was so with the disciples. The Spirit, with whom they were filled, led them to preach Christ as the Crucified One. Later on He led them to glory in the fellowship of the cross, by which they were deemed worthy to suffer for Christ's sake.

How foolish it is to pray for the fullness of the Spirit if we have not first placed ourselves under the full power of the cross. The crucifixion of Christ had touched, broken, and taken possession of the disciples at Pentecost (Acts 2). They could speak or think of nothing else, and when their Savior had shown them His hands and His feet, He said to them, "Receive the Holy Spirit." And so also, with their hearts full of the crucified Christ, now received up into heaven, they were prepared to be filled with the Spirit. They dared to proclaim to the people, "Repent and believe," and they also received the Holy Spirit.

Christ yielded himself unreservedly to the cross. It was the will of His Father. It was the only way to redeem the lost. The cross demands our entire life. To comply with this demand requires nothing less than an act of the will, and for this we are unfit in the natural sense. But if we submit our will to Him who stands waiting to receive us, we will be enabled to do what we could not otherwise do.

—— *Living a Prayerful Life*

THE COMING
REVIVAL

✽

*Wilt thou not revive us again: that thy people may
rejoice in thee?*

Psalm 85:6 KJV

Those who know anything of the history of revivals will remember how often this has been proven: Both widespread and local revivals have been traced to specific prayer. The coming revival will be no exception. An extraordinary spirit of prayer, urging believers to private as well as united prayer, motivating them to labor fervently in their supplications, is a sure sign of approaching showers and even floods of blessing.

Let all who are burdened with a lack of spirituality or with the mediocre state of the life of believers, hear the call that comes to us all: If there is to be revival—a true, divine outpouring of God's Spirit—it will correspond with wholehearted prayer and faith.

No believer should think that he is too weak to help, or imagine that his input would not be missed. If we will only begin, the gift that is in us will become evident and we will become God's intercessor for our own circle of friends, neighborhood, or church body.

Think of the need of souls in general, of the sins and shortcomings among God's people, of the lack of power in preaching. Then begin to cry unto God, "Will you not revive us again that your people may rejoice in you?" Let us allow the truth to press deep into our hearts: Every revival comes, just as Pentecost came, as a direct result of united and continued prayer. So the coming revival must begin with a revival of prayer. It is in the prayer closet, with the door closed, that the sound of abundance of rain will first be heard. An increase of private prayer among our ministers as well as the congregation as a whole is a sure indication of coming blessing.

—— *The Ministry of Intercessory Prayer*

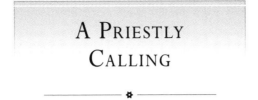

A PRIESTLY CALLING

❋

You also, like living stones, are being built into a spiritual house to be a holy priesthood, offering spiritual sacrifices acceptable to God through Jesus Christ.

1 Peter 2:5

The Spirit gives the power and equips us for believing prayer. He breathes into us the priestly spirit: burning love for God's honor and the saving of souls. He makes us so one with Jesus that prayer in His name is a reality. He strengthens us for believing, persistent prayer. The more the Christian is truly filled with the Spirit of Christ, the more spontaneous will be his life of priestly intercession. Beloved fellow Christians, God needs priests who will draw near to Him, who will live in His presence, and by their intercession bring down the blessing of His grace on a waiting world. The world needs priests who will bear the burden of the perishing and intercede mightily on their behalf.

Are you willing to offer yourself for this work? You know the surrender it demands: nothing less than the Christlike giving up of all so that the saving purposes of God's love may be accomplished among all peoples. Let nothing keep you back from giving yourselves to be wholly and only priests of the Most High God.

The Spirit provides a divine fitness, teaching you to pray according to the will of God. Under the covering of the blood of Christ and His Spirit, you have the assurance that all the wonderful promises concerning prayer in the name of Jesus will be fulfilled in you. Abiding in union with the Great High Priest avails us of the promise, "Anyone who has faith in me will do what I have been doing. . . . And I will do whatever you ask in my name, so that the Son may bring glory to the Father" (John 14:12–13). You will have power to pray the effectual prayer of the righteous man that avails much.

—— *Teach Me to Pray*

165

ROOTED *in* CHRIST

❖

As you therefore have received Christ Jesus the Lord, so walk in Him, rooted and built up in Him and established in the faith, as you have been taught, abounding in it with thanksgiving.

Colossians 2:6–7 NKJV

*I*n these words the apostle teaches us an important lesson: It is not only by faith that we first come to Christ and are united to Him but also by faith that we are to be rooted and established in our union with Christ. Faith is essential not only for the commencement but also for the progress of the spiritual life. Abiding in Jesus can only be by faith.

It is astonishing how such faith will work out all that is further implied in abiding in Christ. There is in the Christian life a great need for watchfulness and prayer, of self-denial, obedience, and diligence. It is faith that continually closes its eyes to the weakness of the creature and finds its joy in the sufficiency of an almighty Savior that makes the soul strong and glad. This faith follows the leading of the Spirit from page to page of the blessed Word with the one desire to take each revelation of what Jesus is and what He promises as its nourishment and its life. You will live "by every word that proceeds from the mouth of God" (Matthew 4:4 NKJV) in accordance with the promise, "Therefore let that abide in you which you heard from the beginning. If what you heard from the beginning abides in you, you also will abide in the Son and in the Father" (1 John 2:24 NKJV).

If you would abide in Christ, only believe. Kneel before your Lord and say to Him in childlike faith: "You are my Vine and I am your branch; I will this day abide in you."

—— *Abiding in Christ*

THE UNCHANGING POWER *of* GOD

✤

We give You thanks, O Lord God Almighty, the One who is and who was and who is to come, because You have taken Your great power and reigned.

Revelation 11:17 NKJV

God's power is wonderful! We see it in creation; we see it in the wonders of redemption recorded in the Old Testament. We see it in the wonderful works of Christ that the Father wrought in Him, and above all, in Christ's resurrection from the dead. We are called on to believe in the Son just as we believe in the Father. Yes, the Lord Jesus, who in His love is so tenderly near us, is the Almighty One with whom nothing is impossible. Whatever may be in our hearts or flesh that will not bow to His will, He can and will conquer. Everything that is promised in God's Word, and all that is our inheritance as children of the new covenant, the Almighty can bestow upon us.

When I bow before Him in prayer, I am in contact with the eternal, unchanging power of God. When I commit myself for the day to the Lord Jesus, I may rest assured that His eternal, almighty power takes me under its protection and accomplishes all for me.

If only we would take time for the hidden place of prayer so that we might experience in full the presence of Jesus, what a blessed life would be ours through faith—an unbroken fellowship with an omnipresent and almighty Lord.

—— Living a Prayerful Life

The readings in this book have been excerpted and adapted from Bethany House Publishers editions of the Andrew Murray classics with the exception of a very early edition of *The Lord's Table* (Moody Press), edited for this book.

* *Abiding in Christ,* 2003

* *Absolute Surrender,* 2003

* *The Believer's Call to Commitment,* 2005

* *The Believer's Daily Renewal,* 2004

* *Believing Prayer,* 2004

* *The Blood of Christ,* 2001

* *Divine Healing,* 2002

* *The Fullness of the Spirit,* 2004

* *Humility,* 2001

* *The Indwelling Spirit,* 2006

* *A Life of Obedience,* 2004

* *Living a Prayerful Life,* 2002

* *The Lord's Table,* undated

* *The Ministry of Intercessory Prayer,* 2003

* *The Path to Holiness,* 2001

* *Raising Your Child to Love God,* 2001

* *Teach Me to Pray,* 2002

* *Waiting on God,* 2001

---- ✿ ----

ANDREW MURRAY was a man wholly consecrated to God. Born in 1828, of missionary parents serving in South Africa, Andrew was blessed with a rich spiritual heritage, a keen intellect, and a happy disposition. His godly father played an important role in his spiritual development and that of his ten siblings. At ten years of age, Andrew and his older brother were sent to study in Aberdeen, Scotland, where they lived with their uncle, a devout Christian minister. Under the godly influence of their uncle and his colleagues, both boys eventually pursued the ministry as their vocation.

During his subsequent years of study at the University of Utrecht, in Holland, Andrew experienced a true spiritual conversion—an encounter that gave him great assurance of a personal relationship with the Lord. Andrew told his father in a letter that he had been "born again."

In 1848, at just twenty years of age, Murray was ordained by the Dutch Reformed Church. His first congregation was located in the frontier town of Bloemfontein, South Africa. While sparsely populated, his parish covered several thousand square miles. In spite of his youth, Andrew quickly won the hearts of the Dutch colonists.

In March 1855, while staying in the home of a godly layman, Andrew became acquainted with the man's daughter, Emma Rutherford. Within a few weeks he had proposed, and they were married in July 1856.

Emma was very accomplished in music, literature, and the arts. A godly woman who loved people, she was well-suited to the ministries of hospitality and pastoral care that she assumed. She and Andrew raised four sons and four daughters.

In 1860, they moved to Worcester to take a new congregation. A revival broke out in that church, which would later be known as the Great Revival of 1860. Respect for Andrew Murray continued to grow within his denomination, and in 1864, he became joint pastor for a large Dutch Reformed church in Cape Town. Besides his pastoral work, he found many expressions for ministry, including social work among the poor, establishing schools, and serving on international church councils. In time, Andrew's exhausting schedule exacerbated his already weakened health, and he was offered a call to a much smaller congregation, which he accepted. From the small parsonage in Wellington, Andrew Murray's ministry spread around the world as he began to set to paper his spiritual insights. His thoughts and ideas concerning the deeper life, church renewal, and revival flowed from his pen like a river, producing many books that were eventually translated into several languages.

Emma died at the age of seventy, in 1905, and Andrew retired from the pastorate the following year, while continuing to write, speak, and travel. Then in 1917, at the age of eighty-eight, Andrew passed into the presence of the Lord.

Murray's messages, which have circled the globe, changing countless lives, are from a man who was both ordinary and extraordinary. The rich legacy of Andrew Murray's life continues to bless people even today. His ageless insights into the kingdom of God encourage us to pursue a deeper life of fellowship with Christ.

✿